Banned Books

Banned Books

Penguin Random House

Produced for DK by Toucan Books

DK LONDON
Senior Editor Victoria Heyworth-Dunne
Senior Designer Mark Cavanagh
Senior US Editor Megan Douglass
Managing Editor Gareth Jones
Senior Managing Art Editor Lee Griffiths
Production Editor Robert Dunn
Senior Production Controller Rachel Ng
Illustrator Emma Fraser Reid
Jacket Design Development Manager
Sophia M.T.T.
Jacket Designer Akiko Kato
Associate Publishing Director Liz Wheeler
Art Director Karen Self
Publishing Director Jonathan Metcalf

DK DELHI
Senior Jackets Designer: Suhita Dharamjit
Senior DTP Designer: Harish Aggarwal
Senior Jackets Coordinator: Priyanka Sharma-Saddi

First American Edition, 2022
Published in the United States by DK Publishing
1745 Broadway, 20th Floor, New York, NY 10018

Copyright © 2022 Dorling Kindersley Limited
DK, a Division of Penguin Random House LLC
23 24 25 26 10 9 8 7 6 5 4 3
004–326786–August/2022

A catalog record for this book
is available from the Library of Congress.
ISBN: 978-0-7440-5628-0

Printed and bound in Slovakia

For the curious
www.dk.com

FSC
www.fsc.org
MIX
Paper | Supporting
responsible forestry
FSC™ C018179

This book was made with Forest
Stewardship Council™ certified
paper – one small step in DK's
commitment to a sustainable future.
For more information go to
www.dk.com/our-green-pledge

Contents

The Postwar Years

The Late 20th Century

The 21st Century

Introduction

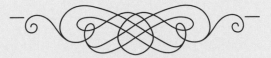

Books have been banned for as long as people have been writing things down. By 1559, the Catholic Church had compiled a list of banned books called the *Index Librorum Prohibitorum* (Index of Prohibited Books). More than 400 years later, in 1989, Iran's Ayatollah Ruhollah Khomeini called for the author of *The Satanic Verses*, Salman Rushdie, to be executed for blasphemy.

Outright bans, in which authorities forbid a book to be published or sold, are not the only form of censorship. Rather, books can be made difficult to access, perhaps by being removed from schools and libraries. Just as insidiously, authors and publishers sometimes censor themselves by not creating or publishing work that might give offense.

The earliest guarantee of freedom of speech was in the Declaration of the Rights of Man and of the Citizen, adopted in 1789 during the French Revolution. Two years later, in the United States, the First Amendment enshrined the same freedom in the Constitution. Despite these guarantees, books have continued to be banned, the rights of readers restricted, and court cases fought.

This book is full of controversial, provocative, and revolutionary literature whose publication, sale, or availability has been curtailed at some point in history. In the long run, such censorship is usually counterproductive. As Mark Twain knew (see page 40), restricting access to a book serves only to create a best seller, because everyone wants to read a book that is forbidden.

Pre-1900

The Decameron

Giovanni Boccaccio

1370s

Giovanni Boccaccio's *The Decameron* is set in 1348, the year the Black Death arrived in Florence. It features 10 young men and women who have fled Florence for a villa in the nearby hills. Over 10 days, they amuse themselves by telling each other 100 stories.

Written in the Tuscan vernacular, the tales were immensely popular, but their content, which was often irreverent, and frequently bawdy, upset Church authorities. On February 7, 1497, a Dominican preacher called Girolamo Savonarola publicly burned *The Decameron* along with other "sinful" books and artworks, an event remembered as the Bonfire of the Vanities. Around 60 years later, Pope Paul IV listed *The Decameron* on the Roman Catholic Church's *Index Librorum Prohibitorum* (Index of Forbidden Books; see page 161) of 1559, condemning the depiction of religious figures engaging in sexual acts.

> **" Nothing is so indecent that it cannot be said to another person if the proper words are used to convey it. "**
>
> **Giovanni Boccaccio**

Although *The Decameron* was officially banned in 1564, copies continued to circulate, so the Church looked for ways to remove the offensive passages. A revised version that replaced the religious characters with other members of society but preserved the sexual references was authorized by Pope Gregory XIII in 1573, but nine years later, Pope Sixtus V ordered the removal of all sexual activity and innuendos from the book. Although this version was published, it did not satisfy Sixtus and remained on the Index.

Complaints regarding the "immoral" nature of *The Decameron* resurfaced in the US in the late 19th century, when public libraries called for a ban of the "indecent" text. Although the US Supreme Court ruled in 1894 that classic texts like *The Decameron* were not considered obscene, various states banned it, and booksellers who owned or sold the text faced harassment and prosecution.

The Canterbury Tales

Geoffrey Chaucer

1387–1400

A cornerstone of English literature, Geoffrey Chaucer's *The Canterbury Tales* presents a multilayered portrait of England in the Middle Ages. It features 31 pilgrims—a cross-section of society—on a four-day journey from London's Tabard Inn to the shrine of St. Thomas Becket in Canterbury Cathedral. On the way, the pilgrims spin tales for each other's edification, amusement, or embarrassment. Their stories, "prologues" (where they introduce themselves to their fellow pilgrims), and many interjections not only reveal their individual characters but also expose a divided society in which corruption and hypocrisy flourish.

Some of the oldest four-letter words in English first saw print in Chaucer's masterpiece. The text bursts with stories of fornication, infidelity, and flatulence. The five-times married Wife of Bath, the only secular female pilgrim in the group, challenges patriarchal expectations,

" The bishops, belike, taking his works but for jests and toys, in condemning other books, yet permitted [Chaucer's] books to be read. "

John Foxe, 1570

boasting of her "mastery" over men and celebrating her sexuality. She uses St. Paul's teachings on marriage and the example of King Solomon, to support her arguments, in mockery of the Church.

Despite its social criticism, especially in the unflattering portrayals of churchmen and women, represented by characters such as the Monk, the Pardoner, and the Summoner, *The Canterbury Tales* was not included on the *Index Librorum Prohibitorum*, the Church's list of prohibited books (see page 161). Over the centuries, however, there were attempts to tone down, abridge, or omit some of the tales. In the 19th and early 20th centuries, sanitized versions of *The Canterbury Tales* were the only ones allowed in the US mail, thanks to the anti-obscenity Comstock laws of 1873, instigated by postal inspector Anthony Comstock—grounds, perhaps, for a "Censor's Tale."

Wycliffe's Bible

John Wycliffe
1382

In 1408, a synod of English clergy meeting in Oxford and presided over by Archbishop Thomas Arundel of Canterbury banned the works of the late Oxford theologian John Wycliffe. Anyone reading Wycliffe's works, including the Wycliffe Bible, could be charged with heresy—dissent from the accepted teachings of the Church. According to a royal statute issued in 1401 by King Henry IV, anyone convicted of heresy could be sentenced to death by being burned "in a high place"—at the stake.

Ordained a priest in 1351, Wycliffe had been a controversial theologian. Naturally cantankerous, he won fame as a plain-speaking opponent of the medieval Church's accumulation of wealth and power. Over time, his attacks became more radical, focusing on fundamental Church beliefs. He insisted that ultimate authority for the Church's core beliefs lay not with the Pope and bishops, but in the Bible. He believed that good preaching allowed ordinary people to access the Bible and form their own judgments. Most controversially, Wycliffe attacked the doctrine of transubstantiation—the belief that bread and wine actually become the body and blood of Christ during the Eucharist. Wycliffe's ideas attracted a growing band of followers, who came to be known as the Lollards, originally a derogatory term, possibly from the Dutch word *lollaert*, meaning "mutterer or mumbler."

The first Wycliffe (or Lollard) Bible was produced in 1382, followed by a revision six years later. Wycliffe himself was not the translator, but it was the importance he attached to scripture that gave rise

A woodcut depicts the translation of the Wycliffe Bible.

to the translation. He wanted ordinary people to be able to read or hear the Bible in their own tongue rather than Latin, the language of the Church and scholarship. The idea was not in itself controversial. Earlier scholars had translated portions of the Bible, including the ninth-century monk Bede, credited with translating John's gospel into Northumbrian English. Roughly contemporary with the Wycliffe (or Lollard) Bible is the Wenceslaus Bible, a translation into German that was commissioned by King Wenceslaus IV of Bohemia.

> " Let the Church of England
> now approve the true and whole
> translation of simple men. "

John Purvey, c. 1388

It was the association with Wycliffe that spelled trouble for the Wycliffe Bible. The principal translators were Wycliffe's associates, Nicholas of Hereford and John Purvey. They were not translating from the Bible's original languages, but from the then-standard Vulgate Bible—itself a fourth-century translation into Latin.

An English Church council in 1382 judged many of Wycliffe's writings either heretical or erroneous. After this, Wycliffe retired from Oxford to his parish of Lutterworth, Leicestershire, where he died in 1384. The Lollards, however, survived, and when Henry IV seized the English throne in 1399, the new king and Arundel, his Archbishop of Canterbury, resolved to suppress them. The first Lollard to be burned at the stake was William Sawtrey, in 1401.

In 1414, Henry's son, the young Henry V, crushed a Lollard revolt led by Herefordshire knight Sir John Oldcastle. The following year, a council of the Western Church meeting by Lake Constance (bordering Germany, Austria, and Switzerland) declared Wycliffe a heretic and ordered his works to be banned and burned throughout Europe. The council also condemned Czech theologian Jan Hus, who had been influenced by Wycliffe. Hus was duly burned at the stake, and a few years later, in 1428, Wycliffe's remains at Lutterworth were exhumed and burned, and his ashes were thrown into the Swift River.

Nonetheless, Wycliffe's writings and, above all, the Bible translation bearing his name, survived. Defiant readers clearly relished the Wycliffe Bible, attested by some 250 copies in varying states of

God's Smuggler

Starting in the 1950s, Dutchman Andrew van der Bijl, armed with his Christian faith and, initially, a Volkswagen Beetle, smuggled millions of Bibles into the Soviet Bloc. While not technically banned, the Bible had no place in the workers' paradise. To talk about it in public marked a person as unreliable, and Bibles brought in from abroad were confiscated. Van der Bijl—"Brother Andrew"—defied this restriction with astonishing success. His initiative became an organization called Open Doors, supporting persecuted Christians worldwide.

> **❝** By this translation, the Scriptures have become vulgar, and they are more available to lay, and even to women who can read, than they were to learned scholars. **❞**

Chronicler Henry Knighton, c. 1390

completion still in existence. All these were hand-copied, but a new technology was emerging that would transform books and reading—the printing press. This and the Protestant Reformation—of which Wycliffe is seen as a forerunner—encouraged a flurry of English translations. William Tyndale's translation of the New Testament from Greek was first published in Germany in 1525, after Henry VIII refused to grant him permission to translate the Bible in England. Eventually arrested for heresy in Antwerp, Tyndale was burned at the stake in Brussels in 1530.

Later translators enjoyed a more tranquil reception. Miles Coverdale's 1535 translation, drawing on Tyndale's work, was the first Bible to be entirely translated into English from the original Hebrew and Greek. Finally, the King James Version—commissioned by James I—appeared in 1611. By then, Catholics, too, had an English Bible, the so-called Douai Bible, a translation of the Vulgate.

Page of a 15th-century illuminated manuscript of Wycliffe's Bible

Dialogue on the Two Chief World Systems

———◇———

Galileo Galilei

1632

Banned by the Roman Inquisition the year after its publication, Italian astronomer Galileo Galilei's *Dialogue on the Two Chief World Systems* remained on the Catholic Church's *Index Librorum Prohibitorum* (Index of Prohibited Books; see page 161) for three centuries. At the time, the accepted understanding of the universe was that the sun, planets, and stars orbited Earth. This was based on the teachings of the Greek philosopher Aristotle and confirmed, it was believed, by the Bible. There was, however, another view, put forward by the Polish astronomer Nicholas Copernicus in 1543, that Earth and other heavenly bodies orbited the sun. The more Galileo studied the heavens, the more convinced he became of the Copernican view.

Emboldened by the election of a friend, Maffeo Barberini, as Pope Urban VIII in 1623, Galileo began work on his *Dialogue*, in which different characters discuss the two "world systems"—Aristotelian and Copernican. Despite his papal friendship, upon its publication Galileo was summoned to Rome to answer charges of heresy. He claimed innocence, saying he had presented the Copernican view only as a hypothesis. Later, he was persuaded to plead guilty in return for leniency. Declared "suspect of heresy"—less severe than outright heresy—he was ordered to recant publicly, and condemned to house arrest for life. He died nine years later at his villa above Florence.

" I have been suspected of heresy ...
of having held and believed that the
sun is the center of the world and
immovable, and that the Earth is
not the center and moves. "

Galileo Galilei, 1633

The Response

Sor Juana Inés de la Cruz

1691

The poet Sor Juana Inés de la Cruz, a nun in the Convent of San Jerónimo, was one of the first notable female writers in 17th-century Mexico (then New Spain). Aristocratic patronage in both Mexico and Spain enabled her to evade censorship, though her gender and preference for secular themes drew criticism from clerics and high-ranking officials, eventually forcing her into self-censorship.

In 1690, Sor Juana delivered a sermon in which she criticized the Biblical scholarship of Father Antonio de Vieyra, a respected Jesuit. The sermon was then published by the Bishop of Puebla without Sor Juana's permission. Writing in the guise of a woman, the bishop added a preface reprimanding Sor Juana for transgressing her place in society and urging her to renounce her secular studies in order to devote herself fully to her faith.

Sor Juana responded publicly with a powerful and lengthy defense of both her work and a woman's right to an education. But "The Response" ("Respuesta") was Sor Juana's last work. Between 1693 and her death in 1695, she renounced her writings and sold her books. After her death, her work quickly went out of circulation until the early 20th century, when she was rediscovered and praised for her revolutionary life and impact on Latin American literature.

Moll Flanders

Daniel Defoe

1722

Widely acclaimed for his desert island classic *Robinson Crusoe* in 1719, English author Daniel Defoe published his other great novel, *Moll Flanders*, anonymously three years later. A rambunctious first-person account of the lowlife "fortunes and misfortunes" of its eponymous heroine, the book is regarded as a key work in the emergence of the English novel. It tells the story of Moll's five marriages (including one, unknowingly, to her brother), her career as a petty London thief and sex worker, her transportation to the American colonies, and her eventual repentance.

A literary reputation was no protection against censorship, however. More than 150 years after publication, *Moll Flanders* fell foul of the Comstock laws, repressive legislation passed by the US Congress in 1873 after lobbying by Anthony Comstock, the founder of the New York Society for the Suppression of Vice. Under the new laws, it became a crime to mail or receive "lascivious," "obscene," or "lewd" publications. Comstock himself was the legislation's most energetic enforcer, responsible, according to some estimates, for the arrest of 3,000 individuals and the destruction of 50 tons (45 metric tons) of printed material.

Although Comstock mainly targeted contemporary fiction, he also cast his eye over the classics. Other works banned by the laws included Aristophanes' ancient Greek comedy *Lysistrata* (in which wives refuse to have sex with their husbands to dissuade them from going to war) and Boccaccio's *Decameron* (see page 10). In the case of *Moll Flanders*, it is easy to see what provoked Comstock's displeasure. The irony is that Defoe, like Comstock, came of dissenting puritan stock, and his works are steeped in the themes of sin and redemption.

The 120 Days of Sodom

❧

Marquis de Sade

1785

On October 22, 1785, the Marquis de Sade, a French aristocrat whose name gave rise to the word "sadism," began writing one of the most controversial books in history: *The 120 Days of Sodom*. The novel follows four men who torture, rape, and murder a group of children, aged 12–15, over the course of four months (the 120 days of the title). De Sade wrote it while incarcerated in the Bastille prison for serious sex crimes against women and children. He kept the 15-yard (14-meter) manuscript rolled up in a copper tube and hidden in a wall.

When de Sade was transferred to an asylum in July 1789, 10 days before the storming of the Bastille—the event that symbolizes the start of the French Revolution—he was forced to leave the unfinished manuscript behind. But it was not lost. It was found and sold to the Marquis de Villeneuve-Trans, and, over a century later, acquired by German sexologist Iwan Bloch. In 1904, Bloch printed a small number of copies to further the understanding of human sexuality. The book found an avid readership and copies began to circulate.

Since its wider publication, various governments have tried to ban the book for its graphic accounts of child rape, torture, and murder. In the 1950s, the French government attempted, but failed, to stop publication of de Sade's collected works. Censorship was more successful in the UK, where translations were banned in the 1950s. Although some British publishers got around this by printing excerpts of de Sade's work, a strict ban was imposed in the late 1960s after newspapers revealed that the child-killer Ian Brady had owned one of de Sade's novels. The ban lasted more than 20 years.

> **"** Prepare your heart and mind for the most impure tale that has ever been written or told since our world began. **"**

The Marquis de Sade, 1785

However, champions of *The 120 Days of Sodom* emerged among intellectuals throughout the 20th century. In France, poet Guillaume Apollinaire considered it a manifesto for total liberty. Philosopher Simone de Beauvoir defended the book as an important philosophical exploration of individualism, and de Sade as expressing the outer extreme of individual desires. In 2016, the book became a Penguin Classic, joining works such as Aristotle's *Ethics* in the British publisher's collection of influential literature.

The 19th Century

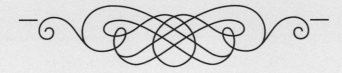

Grimm's Fairy Tales

⟡

The Brothers Grimm

1812

" When I teach my Grimm's
Fairy Tales class, I always say some of
the material contains child abuse,
incest, and other violent material. **"**

Lecturer, Glasgow University, 2019

Brothers Jacob (left) and Wilhelm Grimm, 1847

Many of the world's favorite fairy tales—including Hansel and Gretel, Cinderella, Little Red Riding Hood, Rapunzel, Sleeping Beauty, and Snow White and the Seven Dwarves—are German folk tales gathered and published as *Kinder-und Hausmärchen* (*Nursery and Household Tales*) by brothers Jacob and Wilhelm Grimm in the early 19th century. By the time the seventh and final edition of the book came out in 1857, it was known in English-speaking countries as *Grimm's Fairy Tales*.

At the end of the 19th century, the book ranked second only to the Bible in German homes, where it helped shape an emerging folk culture. The Nazi regime politicized the tales to stir up nationalism and hatred of "non-Aryans," claiming Little Red Riding Hood, for example, symbolized Aryan triumph over the "wolfish Jew."

When the Allies occupied Germany after World War II, the tales were banned in German schools because of their manipulation by the Nazis. Recent debate has focused on the impact the tales, which are often frightening and offensive, could have on young readers; some teachers recommend that they come with a content warning.

Frankenstein

Mary Shelley

1818

Mary Shelley's Gothic fantasy about the scientist Victor Frankenstein and the creature he summons into life from a collection of bones and other material has inspired a whole genre of science fiction horror—not to mention numerous films. Conceived after a half-waking nightmare on the shores of Lake Geneva where Mary and her husband, the Romantic poet Percy Shelley, were spending the summer of 1816 with Lord Byron, the novel received mixed reviews. Some critics found it disturbing; others, such as Sir Walter Scott, praised the author's "original genius."

In the 1950s, *Frankenstein* was banned by South Africa's apartheid regime. A law passed by the South African parliament in 1955 gave the country's customs authorities the right to prohibit any imported publication deemed "indecent or obscene or on any ground whatsoever objectionable." Anyone found in possession of such a work was liable to a large fine or up to five years in prison.

The list of banned publications grew over the years. It included left-wing and anti-racist works, but Mary Shelley's novel also kept company with more surprising publications, including the Victorian children's classic *Black Beauty* (whose title alone was offensive to the racist authorities); Ray Bradbury's *Fahrenheit 451*; Ian Fleming's *The Spy Who Loved Me*, and the Hopalong Cassidy western stories of Louis L'Amour. By the late 1960s, some 13,000 titles featured on the list. Confiscated works were burned weekly in municipal incinerators or sometimes in industrial facilities, such as the furnaces of the state-owned steel company Iscor. The banning of books in South Africa stopped only with the passing of the Publications and Entertainment Act of 1996 following the end of the apartheid regime.

The History of Mary Prince

Mary Prince

1831

When it came out in London in 1831, Mary Prince's heart-rending story of her life as an enslaved Black woman in Britain's West Indian colonies was a publishing sensation. The book was reprinted three times that year alone. Never before had there been such a graphic account of what it was like to be enslaved, even though the book does not reveal the full horror.

At the time, Britain was being torn apart by the slavery debate, and the book provoked a backlash. In a scathing article in *Blackwood's Magazine*, pro-slavery activist James MacQueen denounced it as biased and exaggerated. He also made insulting references to the family of the book's editor, Thomas Pringle, secretary of the Anti-Slavery Society, in whose household Mary had found refuge. Pringle sued *Blackwood's Magazine* and won. At the same time, however, he was sued for defamation by Mary's former enslaver, John Wood of Antigua. Unable to bring witnesses from Antigua, Pringle lost.

Nonetheless, the book survived in print and, like other slave narratives, helped mobilize public opinion against slavery. In August 1833, six months after Pringle's two legal cases came to court, the British Parliament passed the Anti-Slavery Act, abolishing slavery in the British Empire. Sadly, nobody knows what happened to Mary after that. She disappears from the records.

The Communist Manifesto

Karl Marx & Friedrich Engels

1848

" The theory of the Communists may be summed up in the single sentence: Abolition of private property. "

Karl Marx and Friedrich Engels

ДА ЗДРАВСТВУЕТ МАРКСИЗМ-ЛЕНИНИЗМ!

A poster shows (from left) Marx, Engels, and Lenin over the slogan "Long live Marxist-Leninism."

A work that argues openly for revolution—"the forcible overthrow of all existing social conditions"—is likely to fall foul of the authorities, and *The Communist Manifesto* has often been banned. It was prohibited in 19th-century Prussia and imperial Germany, and the Nazis burned it. It has also been banned in parts of the US, especially during the 1950s; a ban in Turkey was not lifted until 2013.

The concept of communism as an egalitarian ideal was widely known by the 1840s, but the manifesto's authors, German exiles Karl Marx and Friedrich Engels, believed it was not an ideal but an inevitable process. They argued that concentrating wealth and power in the hands of the bourgeoisie reduced workers—the proletariat—to mere "instruments of labor." Eventually, they argued, the proletariat would rise up and overthrow their oppressors. In Germany, a legal loophole enabled them to publish a new edition of *Manifesto* in 1872. Its time had come. By the outbreak of World War I in 1914, hundreds of editions had been printed in more than 30 languages.

Leaves of Grass

Walt Whitman

1855

The first edition of American poet Walt Whitman's *Leaves of Grass* was just 12 poems and a long preface in which Whitman sets forth his vision of America as a new Eden. To Whitman, America itself was one vast poem, and the poet the incarnation of America. The collection was reissued six times between 1855 and 1881. Each edition included revised as well as new poems; the final version contained 383 poems.

Besides the (frequently homoerotic) sexual passages throughout the poems, Whitman's aggressively intimate tone violated norms of 19th-century decorum and offended many readers. Whitman called himself "the caresser of life wherever moving" and the poet-speaker in the work declaims that he is "turbulent, fleshy, sensual, eating, drinking, and breeding." He refers frankly to his bowels and to semen. The poem also ignores class distinctions, referring to sex workers and the gentility with equal respect.

The book was decried in press reviews and, in Boston in 1882, explicitly banned. Yielding to pressure from societies for the prevention of vice, libraries and bookshops declined to stock the work. An 1860 review in *The Literary Gazette* suggested an appropriate title for the book would be "Squeals from the Sty."

" If possible, he is more reckless and vulgar than in his two former publications. "

The New York Times, 1860

Walt Whitman, by Samuel Hollyer, 1854

Another contemporary reviewer advised Whitman to find a secluded Long Island cove and drown himself. In 1870, the president of Yale University, Noah Porter, compared Whitman's offense in *Leaves of Grass* to walking naked through the streets. However, not all the reviews were negative, and the epochal nature of the collection was recognized by Ralph Waldo Emerson, Henry David Thoreau, Bronson Alcott, and Oscar Wilde among other contemporary artists and philosophers.

Madame Bovary

Gustave Flaubert

1856

" Madame Bovary has
made a lot of racket with her
first steps in the world. "

L'Illustration, 1857

Gustave Flaubert's first novel, *Madame Bovary*, is acknowledged as one of the great works of 19th-century French literature. At the time of its publication, however, it drew a stern response from the regime of Emperor Napoleon III. Affronted by its frank depiction of the foolish romantic Emma Bovary; her boredom with her doctor husband; her adulterous affairs; and her eventual death by suicide, which is described in graphic detail, the authorities took legal action to ban the book.

The novel nearly slipped past the authorities unnoticed. As was usual, it first appeared in installments, in the literary magazine *Revue de Paris*. Near the end of the serialization, however, the magazine's editor, fearing a backlash, wanted to cut what might be regarded as offensive passages. An annoyed Flaubert vented his feelings to a journalist acquaintance, and this inadvertently alerted the government. At the end of 1856, Flaubert, the *Revue*'s editor, and its printer were summoned to appear before a tribunal, charged with offending public morality, religion, and decency.

The trial started in late January 1857. The state prosecutor accused Flaubert of a lack of decorum, pointing out that although the events described in the novel no doubt took place in French society, it was not the role of literature to portray them so graphically. Fortunately for Flaubert and his fellow accused, the defense lawyer was one of the most experienced advocates in Paris. He demolished the prosecution case, and the three men were acquitted, though not awarded costs.

Madame Bovary could still have been lost to the world, however. Dispirited by the experience, Flaubert contemplated not publishing the novel in book form. In the end, pressure from his mother and his publisher changed his mind. *Madame Bovary* appeared as a book in April 1857.

Poster from the 1949 film *Madame Bovary*

On the Origin of Species by Means of Natural Selection

Charles Darwin

1859

B y 1859, Charles Darwin was a prominent and well-respected naturalist, and the publication of his book *On the Origin of Species by Means of Natural Selection* was eagerly anticipated in the scientific community and beyond. From the outset, however, the book divided scientific opinion, as well as wider society. Many of those who read and understood the book realized that its ideas were revolutionary. Others believed it to be heretical, striking at the heart of traditional Christian beliefs. Although most scientists have long considered it to be the foundation of evolutionary biology, it remains controversial, and the subject of harsh criticism and bans in some countries.

The theory articulated in *On the Origin of Species* had its embryo in Darwin's experiences on the HMS *Beagle* expedition to South America, which he joined as a "gentleman naturalist" and geologist in 1831. He collected thousands of fossils, plants, and animals on the voyage, and continued his research when he returned to Britain in 1836. By the following year, he had pretty much formulated his ideas about evolution, which were rooted in many detailed observations. Famously, he believed the existence of similar, but slightly different, bird species (later dubbed "Darwin's finches") on different islands in the Galapagos archipelago could only be explained if "one species does change into another." The idea of evolution from one species to another was not new, but Darwin produced a plausible mechanism by which it could happen.

> ## " It is harmful, as well as groundless. "
> **William Jennings Bryan**, 1922

On the Origin of Species explains Darwin's theory of evolution. He argues that as there is competition for resources (primarily food) and individual members of a species vary in their ability to feed—for example, some are faster, or have sharper eyesight—some will fare better than others. Those that do are more likely to live long enough to breed and pass on their attributes. Because those with weaker traits are less likely to survive and breed, individuals with the stronger attributes gradually come to dominate the population.

Darwin called this process natural selection, and concluded that it resulted in species that are better adapted to their environment. Natural selection eventually produced plants and animals that were different from their ancestors—new species.

A Christian himself, Darwin initially delayed publishing his work, fearing how it would be viewed by the Church and aware that he might be associated with seditious atheists. It was only when he learned that fellow zoologist Alfred Russel Wallace had arrived at

Charles Darwin caricatured on the front page of the French satirical magazine *La Petite Lune*, 1878

" High authorities pronounce the whole thing to be positively mischievous. "

Asa Gray, 1860

similar conclusions and was planning to publish them that he decided to act. Independent papers by Darwin and Wallace were read at a meeting of the Linnean Society in London in July 1858 but received little attention. However, when *On the Origin of Species* went on sale the following year, its first print run of 1,250 sold out in a day. By the end of the century, more than 100,000 copies had been sold.

The theory sparked bitter controversy because it challenged the Christian tenets that God had created each species separately and implied that *Homo sapiens* had evolved from primates, denying humans their special place in God's plan.

Academic, geologist, and Anglican priest Adam Sedgwick led the opposition to the book at Cambridge University, where William Whewell banned it from the library of Trinity College. In the Oxford Debate of 1860, Bishop of Oxford Samuel Wilberforce and biologist Thomas Huxley argued over the book's veracity. Wilberforce, a strong opponent of the work, asked Huxley whether it was through his grandfather or his grandmother that he claimed his descent from a monkey (Huxley allegedly said he would rather have an ape in his ancestry than the bishop, who wasted his time ridiculing an important scientific discussion). Nonetheless, neither the Church of England nor the Catholic Church tried to ban *On the Origin of Species*, though it was banned in Yugoslavia in 1935, Greece in 1937, and Malaysia in 2006. Fundamentalist Christian organizations in the US have had some success in excluding Darwin's ideas from the school curriculum.

The "Monkey Trial"

In 1925, the passage of the Butler Bill in the US state of Tennessee banned the teaching of evolution, opposing the idea that "man has descended from a lower order of animals." Later that year, science teacher John Scopes was found guilty of breaking the law and fined $100 in a hearing dubbed the "Monkey Trial" because of the contention that humans evolved from primates. Although Scopes's sentence was quashed on a technicality, the Tennessee ban on teaching Darwin's ideas in schools remained until 1967. In fact, school boards across the US continue to debate how to teach theories about the origins of life on Earth.

Adventures of Huckleberry Finn

Mark Twain

1885

Mark Twain in his publisher's office c.1900.

An American classic, Mark Twain's coming-of-age novel *Adventures of Huckleberry Finn* is one of the most frequently challenged books in the US. First removed from libraries in Massachusetts three months after its publication in 1885, it remains controversial today. Many reasons have been given for censoring the book over the years. Its positive depiction of the friendship between Huck, a white child, and Jim, an enslaved Black man, upset some white readers when it was first published; the infantilization of Jim and other Black characters offends Black readers; and its use of the N-word more than 200 times makes it uncomfortable reading for most people and gravely offensive to many Black Americans.

Set in the American South before the abolition of slavery, the story centers on two outcasts who become unlikely friends. Huck, a white boy, is running away from his father (a violent drunk) and society; Jim is an enslaved man seeking freedom. After encountering one another on an island in the Mississippi River where they are both hiding, they set off by raft to Ohio, a free state (where slavery is illegal). Along the way, Huck learns from Jim's wisdom and generosity.

The book is told in the first person by Huck, who has been taught that an enslaved person is the property of their enslaver. But as Huck gets to know Jim, his views change. After wrestling with the doctrines instilled by his upbringing, he decides to help Jim, even though he is breaking the law—the Fugitive Slave Act of 1850—by not reporting him to the authorities, saying, "All right then, I'll go to hell."

Like Huck, Mark Twain (1835–1910) grew up in Missouri. His father and uncle enslaved Black people, and during the Civil War, Twain served in the Confederate Army for two weeks before

> " They have expelled Huck from their library as 'trash and suitable only for the slums.' That will sell 25,000 copies for us. "

Mark Twain, 1885

deserting. However, as an adult, Twain changed his ideas and went on to espouse equal rights for Black Americans; to pay for a Black student to attend Yale University; and to write *Huckleberry Finn*, which he intended as an attack on racism. Although the author often depicts Black characters in the book, including Jim, as superstitious and childish, Jim is also its most admirable character. By contrast, most of the white characters are violent, ignorant, selfish, and hypocritical.

Huckleberry Finn used to be banned in the USSR and China, but it is its censorship history in the US that is most controversial. Until recently, it was the only book most American students ever encountered in the curriculum that had a Black main character, that was written in Southern vernacular English, and that tackled the subject of racism and slavery. The satire and first-person narration require careful teaching so that their seeming racism is challenged in classroom discussions and Black students' concerns are recognized. Many Black American parents are unconvinced that teachers are doing this, and they do not want their children to be put in the difficult position of either having to say the N-word or refusing to say it when called upon to read aloud in class. This has led some parents and educators to demand the removal of the book from the curriculum. Other teachers recommend that it is taught only in the last two years of high school, when students have the maturity to understand the subtleties of the text and discussions of the book can lead to a broader awareness of the impact of race and racism in America.

Removing the N-Word

A professor at Auburn University in Alabama, sought to make *Huckleberry Finn* more palatable to modern students by replacing all 213 instances of the N-word with the term "slave" in a 2011 edition of the novel. Professor Alan Gribben also replaced the offensive "Injun" with "Indian." But some commentators questioned whether it was right to sanitize the book, arguing that Twain intended to educate readers by shocking them with these vile words. Others claim that replacing these words does not solve the underlying racism shown in the portrayal of the Black characters.

" The N-word sums up
for us who are colored all
the bitter years of insult
and struggle in America. "

Langston Hughes, 1940

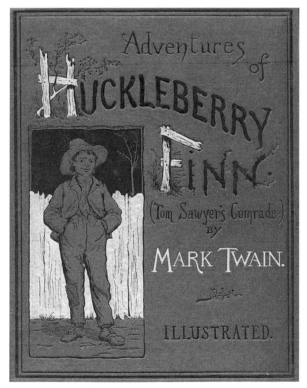

The cover of an early edition of *Huckleberry Finn*

The Earth

Émile Zola

1887

Avivid portrait of French peasant life, with coarse language and explicit sex scenes, Émile Zola's novel *La Terre* (*The Earth*), the 15th novel in his Rougon-Macquart series, alienated many readers when it was published in 1887. In a "manifesto" printed in *Le Figaro* newspaper, five former supporters of Zola's work deplored his descent into the "depths of filth."

It was the author's English publisher, Henry Vizetelly, however, who faced legal action. When he issued a translation of *La Terre*, as *The Soil*, in 1888, the National Vigilance Association, affronted by the novel's sex scenes—and one in which a woman gives birth next to a cow delivering a calf, blurring the difference between human and animal—took Vizetelly to court for obscenity. Advised to plead guilty, the publisher was fined £100 and agreed to withdraw the translation.

Vizetelly had an obstinate streak, however, and reissued the book the following year, albeit without the offending sections. Back in court, he was fined £200 and given a three-month prison sentence. It was an experience from which the 69-year-old publisher never fully recovered, and he died in 1894. Zola outlived him by eight years, during which he completed two more series of novels.

The Awakening

Kate Chopin

1899

C ited as an early feminist text, Kate Chopin's *The Awakening* draws attention to women's oppression in the US South in the late 19th century through the story of one woman's experiences. Edna Pontellier, a married woman with children, questions her life upon meeting and falling in love with a younger man—Robert Lebrun. Her awakening prompts her to seek a life of independence outside the constrained roles of wife and mother, the type of autonomy that was frowned on in the patriarchal society in which Chopin lived and wrote.

Reviewers balked at *The Awakening* upon its publication. They wrote that Edna Pontellier was a "selfish" character and took issue with the book's critique of prescribed roles for women, its unapologetic female sexuality, and the suicide—the only way Edna saw herself becoming free—at its climax. The negative response to the novel had serious consequences for Chopin. Frowned on by society, she was prevented from joining the St. Louis Fine Arts Club, and her once-flourishing career came to a standstill. She struggled to find publishers for new stories, which she had previously placed in leading magazines, and a third collection of stories was canceled by her publisher. In 1902, *The Awakening* was removed from a library in Evanston, Illinois. Two years after this, Chopin died of a brain hemorrhage.

As second-wave feminism took off in the 1960s and '70s, Chopin's talent was rediscovered, and *The Awakening* entered the canon as one of the earliest and finest works of modern feminist literature. To date, her work has been translated into more than 20 languages and continues to touch countless women yearning for autonomy. Nonetheless, as recently as 2006, a school board attempted (and failed) to ban *The Awakening* from six affiliated schools in Arlington Heights, Chicago, for depicting "sexual situations inappropriate for students."

Between the Wars

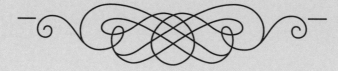

Ulysses

James Joyce

1922

" All the secret sewers of vice are canalized in [*Ulysses's*] flood of unimaginable thoughts, images, and pornographic words. "

James Douglas, *The Sunday Express*, 1922

Irish author James Joyce's stream-of-consciousness masterpiece *Ulysses* follows a day in the lives of three characters—Stephen Dedalus, Leopold Bloom, and Bloom's wife Molly—as they go about their business in Dublin. It draws on Homer's epic poem *The Odyssey*, but its characters are concerned with the nitty-gritty details of their lives, revealed through internal monologues. These include a sexually explicit 22,000-word soliloquy by Molly at the end of the book.

From 1918, the novel began to appear in installments in *The Little Review*, a US literary magazine, but when the publication's editors were convicted of obscenity, it looked as if the work might never get published in its entirety. Eventually, Sylvia Beach, the American founder of Shakespeare and Company, a bookshop in Paris, wrote to Joyce begging the "honor of bringing out your *Ulysses*." In 1922, she printed 1,000 copies, which were smuggled around the world.

In 1932, Random House in New York challenged the ban and imported a single copy. At the trial that duly followed, the judge ruled that *Ulysses* was not obscene, a decision that was upheld on appeal. Random House published the first legal edition of *Ulysses* in the US in 1934. In Britain, The Bodley Head followed suit in 1936.

Sylvia Beach and James Joyce at her bookshop in Paris

Mein Kampf

Adolf Hitler

1925

In the mid-1920s, Adolf Hitler's two-volume outpouring of hatred and rage, *Mein Kampf* ("My Struggle") had few admirers; critics found it tedious and gave it poor reviews. Yet after 1933, when Hitler was elected Chancellor of Germany, *Mein Kampf* became a nationwide best-seller, prominently displayed in every bookstore, every house, and every classroom in the Third Reich. The state gave all newly married couples a copy of the book as a wedding present.

Even then, until 1939, when it was published in English and other languages, few people outside Germany read *Mein Kampf*. Those who did were alarmed at Hitler's intention for world domination by a white "Aryan" race. The book presented the blueprint for genocide that Hitler followed during World War II (1939–1945), when 50–60 million people died worldwide and an estimated 5.7 million Jewish people, and countless Roma, LGBTQ+, and disabled people, among others, were murdered in Europe. Baron Elwyn-Jones, a counsel at the Nuremberg Trials, said, "From *Mein Kampf* the way leads directly to the furnaces of Auschwitz and the gas chambers of Majdanek."

After the war, many countries restricted the sale or display of *Mein Kampf*. In Germany, Bavaria—the state that inherited the copyright after Hitler's suicide—refused to permit its publication, and it was only after the book came into the public domain in 2015 that a heavily annotated scholarly edition of the work was published in the country. In 2020, Amazon announced that it would no longer sell copies of the book because its content violated the company's code of conduct. However, the company then reinstated the book, saying it "served an important educational role in understanding and preventing antisemitism." The debate continues, with some people claiming that publication exposes Hitler's lies. A number of Jewish groups have long called for the book's outright ban.

Elmer Gantry

Sinclair Lewis

1927

This satirical novel rocked America in the late 1920s, and the name Elmer Gantry is still a byword for people who do not practice what they preach. It tells the story of a failed minister (Gantry) who becomes a traveling salesman in America's Midwest. When he meets Sister Sharon Falconer, a touring evangelist, he falls for her and becomes an integral part of her sermons, acting the part of a traveling salesman who finds God. The ultimate hypocrite, Gantry goes on to make a fortune preaching a faith he does not believe in and attacking all the vices he does possess—adultery, alcohol, and avarice.

When *Elmer Gantry* came out in 1927, ministers called for it to be banned. The well-known evangelist Billy Sunday (who had appeared in one of Lewis's other novels as the Reverend Monday) called Lewis "Satan's cohort." The book was banned in Boston; Kansas City, Missouri; and elsewhere, and a copy was burned in Ohio. News of the bans fueled sales and the book became America's best-selling novel of the year.

Lady Chatterley's Lover

D. H. Lawrence
1928

L*ady Chatterley's Lover* (1928) was British novelist D. H. Lawrence's final and most notorious novel. His previous novels had also been censored to a degree, but *Lady Chatterley*, with its explicit sex scenes between an aristocratic woman and a working-class gamekeeper, created a colossal scandal in Britain. The country's publishers would not touch the book, so Lawrence had 1,000 copies privately printed in Italy. These soon sold out, providing much-needed income for the author.

Lawrence was aware that his novel was explosive and calmly stood by *Lady Chatterley*, declaring that he was "perfectly content" to endure the condemnation of the offended. He did not live to see the publication of an unexpurgated version of the novel, because he died of tuberculosis in 1930, at the age of 44.

The plot of *Lady Chatterley's Lover* centers on an adulterous love affair between Lady Constance Chatterley and Oliver Mellors, the gamekeeper on the Chatterley country estate. Sir Clifford, Lady Chatterley's husband, has returned from World War I paralyzed from the waist down and is impotent. The sex scenes between Lady Chatterley and Mellors are rendered in florid detail and express Lawrence's view that sexual intercourse is a type of natural sacrament.

The interclass relationship in the novel reflects the author's own experience: born within walking distance of the Nottinghamshire coal mines, where his father and uncles worked, Lawrence married Frieda Weekley (née von Richthofen), the daughter of a German baron. The marriage, which endured until Lawrence's death, was open—Frieda is known to have taken other lovers.

" I enjoyed ... dropping a little bomb in the world's crinoline of hypocrisy. "

D. H. Lawrence, 1928

Lady Chatterley was published in the US before the UK. Although imports of the novel to the US had been banned in 1929, in 1959, a federal judge permitted its publication on grounds of literary merit, a decision upheld on appeal. Barney Rosset, the head of Grove Press, its US publisher, said he had fought for *Lady Chatterley* with the explicit intention of opening the gates for other censored books, such as Henry Miller's *Tropic of Cancer*.

In 1960, Penguin Books published *Lady Chatterley* in the UK and was immediately taken to court by the Director of Public Prosecutions, on the grounds that the novel was obscene. It was a test case of the 1959 Obscene Publications Act, which had replaced an older, more draconian law and included a loophole—the publication of material that might otherwise be considered obscene was allowed if it was "in the interests of science, literature, art, or learning." Witnesses in defense of *Lady Chatterley* included Dame Helen Gardner, fellow of St. Hilda's College, Oxford (who replied "Oh no!" when asked if she would hesitate to lecture on the novel to undergraduates); the novelist Dame Rebecca West; the Bloomsbury novelist E. M. Forster; and the Bishop of Woolwich, who declared that Lawrence's view of sex celebrated the sanctity of organic relationships.

Britain's middle and upper classes were largely horrified at the thought that a member of the aristocracy would have a sexual relationship with a working-class lover. The trial prosecutor, Mervyn Griffith-Jones, alluded to the implicit threat to the British status quo when he asked the jury, "Is this a book you would wish your wife or servants to read?" Especially concerning to many of the book's critics was the fact that Penguin had priced the paperback book at a mere three shillings and sixpence (the price of a few cigarettes), making it affordable to the lower classes.

There was close textual review and analysis of the work in court. The prosecutor helpfully supplied the jury with an itemized report of every frank sexual word used in the text; meanwhile, the wife of presiding judge Sir Laurence Byrne hand-annotated a copy of the text for her spouse, noting "lovemaking" or "coarse" at relevant places in the book's margin.

In the end, the jury took just three hours to render a verdict of not guilty. Within days, more than 200,000 copies of the novel had been purchased, and sales figures reached 3 million within a few months. *Lady Chatterley's Lover* was Lawrence's most commercially successful novel.

Repeat offender

Lady Chatterley's Lover was not the first of Lawrence's novels to offend the British censors. His 1915 novel, *The Rainbow*, was banned for obscenity two months after publication. Its publisher, Methuen, apologized in court for publishing the novel, stating that it had not sufficiently scrutinized the final version of the text. The most objectionable passage portrayed the sexual encounter of Ursula, the heroine, with a female schoolteacher. Methuen was made to pay the costs of destroying more than 1,000 copies of the novel, and the publisher was chastised by the court for allowing their reputation to be sullied.

Cover of the first British paperback edition, 1960

> " The words themselves are clean,
> so are the things to which they
> apply, but the mind drags in a filthy
> association. Well, then, cleanse the
> mind, that is the real job. "

D. H. Lawrence, 1929

The Well of Loneliness

Radclyffe Hall

1928

Radclyffe Hall's *The Well of Loneliness* centers on the female protagonist Stephen Gordon, an upper-class English tomboy who feels different from other people from an early age. She comes to understand herself as an "invert," a term used in late 19th- and early 20th-century Europe to refer to gay, bi, and trans people, since same-sex attraction was understood as a gendered inversion. Stephen—given a boy's name by her parents who had wanted a son—goes on to pursue Mary Llewellyn, whom she meets while working as an ambulance driver during World War I. Stephen's story is ultimately an unhappy one, and Hall uses the semiautobiographical tale to plead for society's toleration of "inverts."

Although *The Well of Loneliness* is generally recognized as the first lesbian novel, some readers view Stephen as a transgender man rather than a lesbian, citing her assertion that she has always felt like a boy, her preference for boys' and then men's clothing, and her predisposition to engage in "male" habits and behavior.

The book's language is never explicit: apart from kissing, sexual activity is barely described. Nonetheless, the editor of Britain's *Sunday Express* claimed that it could corrupt the vulnerable. When the novel's publisher, Jonathan Cape, tried to enlist the support of the Home

> " I have put my pen at the service of some of the most persecuted and misunderstood people in the world. "

Radclyffe Hall, 1928

Secretary against the newspaper, the plan backfired: the book was castigated for promoting "unnatural offenses" between women, and Hall and her publisher were prosecuted under the Obscene Publications Act of 1857. After a seven-day trial, magistrate Sir Henry Chartres Biron ruled that the book was obscene and ordered its destruction. Hall's reputation never recovered.

Despite the dehumanization faced by Hall, *The Well of Loneliness* has stood the test of time as an iconic text, eventually appearing in several editions and countries. It has lit the way to self-understanding for generations of LGBTQ+ people, especially lesbians, bisexual women, non-binary people, and trans people, though some object to the way it presents their lives as full of suffering.

A Farewell to Arms

Ernest Hemingway

1929

A love story set in Italy during World War I, *A Farewell to Arms* was American author Ernest Hemingway's first major success as a novelist. It was based on his wartime experiences as a volunteer ambulance driver on the Italian front.

The novel's depictions of sex and its salacious language caused consternation when it was published in the US in 1929. Two issues of *Scribner's Magazine*, where it was serialized, were banned in Boston, although the chief effect of this was to boost sales elsewhere. In Italy, Fascist dictator Benito Mussolini, outraged by the book's account of Italian military incompetence, imposed a national ban, though he may also have been partly motivated by Hemingway's description of him as "the biggest bluff in Europe" in an article published by the *Toronto Daily Star* several years earlier.

In the novel, the hero, Frederic Henry, an American ambulance driver serving in the Italian army, falls in love with an English nurse named Catherine Barkley, who goes on to care for him when he is wounded. Eventually forced back to the front, Henry joins the ignominious Italian retreat from Caporetto in October 1917. For Italians, Caporetto was a national humiliation, in which more than 600,000 soldiers deserted or surrendered to the Austro-German forces. Hemingway described the chaos during the retreat in unsparing detail.

The novel's ban in Italy lasted until the late stages of World War II, by which time Mussolini was little more than a Nazi puppet. In 1944, when Nazi officials discovered that a Turin publisher had contracted the writer and translator Fernanda Pivano to produce an

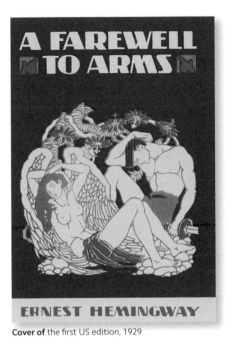

Cover of the first US edition, 1929

Italian edition of *A Farewell to Arms*, the SS briefly arrested and jailed her, threatening dire consequences if she went ahead with the commission. When the war was over, Pivano and Hemingway became friends, and her translation of the novel was published in 1949.

> ❝ [*A Farewell to Arms*] isn't at all erotic, although love is represented as having a very large physical element. ❞

Max Perkins, Hemingway's editor, 1929

All Quiet on the Western Front

Erich Maria Remarque

1929

No novel about World War I has attracted more readers than *All Quiet on the Western Front*. Its young author, Erich Maria Remarque, had served in the German army, and his depiction of trench warfare was so realistic that the book became a worldwide bestseller. Strongly anti-war, it was nominated for the 1931 Nobel Peace Prize.

In Germany, Adolf Hitler and the rising Nazi Party denounced the book for being defeatist. Its depiction of German soldiers as unheroic ran counter to the myth of Teutonic invincibility. In December 1930, when the Academy Award–winning film of the novel was showing in German cities, Nazi Brownshirts disrupted audiences by releasing mice and stink bombs, and attacking anybody thought to be Jewish. Within a week, the Weimar government had banned the film altogether.

After Hitler became chancellor of Germany in 1933, university students sacked libraries and bookstores across the Third Reich and burned tens of thousands of blacklisted books. *All Quiet on the Western Front* was one of them. Although more than a million had been sold in Germany, all remaining copies were turned over to the Gestapo. German-dominated Austria and Mussolini's Italy also banned the novel.

The Nazis, however, also sought revenge. Remarque had left Europe for the US before the outbreak of World War II, but his sister Elfriede had stayed in Germany. She was arrested and beheaded in 1943 in gruesome retaliation.

As I Lay Dying

William Faulkner
1930

American author William Faulkner's tour-de-force *As I Lay Dying* is narrated by 15 characters related to (and including) Addie Bundren, the dying person of the title. It begins when Addie is still alive—and watching her son build her coffin—but most of the novel focuses on the thoughts and interactions of Addie's family after her death, when they take her body to a family burial plot 40 miles (64 km) away in order to honor a promise. As the wagon progresses, battling floods and fire, the coffin becomes increasingly odoriferous.

As I Lay Dying is by turn grotesque, darkly comedic, moving, and horrifying—not unlike the incomprehensible fact of death itself. It was hailed by critics upon publication and helped Faulkner win the 1949 Nobel Prize for Literature.

The novel took decades to percolate down to the high school English class, where it occasionally landed in trouble, especially with school boards in Kentucky. After a complaint by a parent, Graves County School Board banned it in 1986 because it was "offensive and obscene," citing in particular the attempt by Addie's daughter Dewey Dell, who is pregnant, to obtain an abortion. When the case was brought to the attention of the American Civil Liberties Union (ACLU), the county rescinded the ban a week later, in fear of a lawsuit.

In 1987, the novel was challenged in Pulaski County for its "profanity and a segment about masturbation," and a Louisville school tried banning it in 1994 for questioning the existence of God. In wealthy Carroll County, Maryland, the book was challenged for "coarse language and dialect"—two characteristics that help make *As I Lay Dying* relatable and understandable.

Brave New World

Aldous Huxley

1932

Cover of the first edition, 1932

“ Under a scientific dictator ...
most men and women will grow
up to love their servitude and
will never dream of revolution. ”

Aldous Huxley, 1932

In *Brave New World*, British novelist Aldous Huxley rounds on utopian hopes for a technology-driven future. Published in 1932, it depicts a world-state where science and assembly lines have so thoroughly merged that all babies are decanted from test tubes, genetically engineered and postnatally conditioned to fit slots in a caste system.

Superficially, it is a blissful world. Casual sex is abundant; virtual-reality films are very entertaining; and "soma," a happy drug, is always available. The fact that all this is used to control people is lost on everyone except a few "savages," the only ones who struggle and grow old, dare to fall in love, and give birth to children they cherish— the only ones who live meaningful human lives.

The irony and satire were lost on many readers. Ireland, practically a theocracy, banned the book soon after publication, and over the years it has been challenged as classroom reading in the US states of Missouri, Oklahoma, California, Alabama, Idaho, and Texas, primarily for its "adult themes." Most attempts at censorship have failed, however, and the book remains on the shelves of school libraries.

Tropic of Cancer

Henry Miller

1934

" I had read the most terrible, the
most sordid, the most magnificent
manuscript that had ever fallen
into my hands; nothing I had
yet received was comparable to it. "

Jack Kahane, 1939

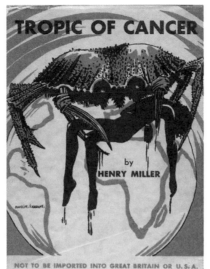

Cover of the first edition of *Tropic of Cancer*, published in Paris in 1934

With its frank descriptions of sex, Henry Miller's first published novel, *Tropic of Cancer*, was banned for obscenity in the US and the UK from its publication in 1934 until the 1960s. The first-person narrative of the day-to-day life of an expatriate American writer in the bohemian world of 1930s Paris is strongly autobiographical. Mingled with the sex and partying are passages of ironic reflection, where the narrator muses upon his life and aspirations as a creative artist.

Born in Brooklyn, New York, the 38-year-old Miller arrived in Paris in 1930, after years of failed attempts at publishing fiction and a succession of jobs. Paris gave him the inspiration he longed for, and he plunged into life there, enjoying a series of affairs, notably with the French-born Cuban-American writer Anaïs Nin. He also became friends with an Englishman called Jack Kahane, owner of the Paris-based Obelisk Press. Kahane specialized in publishing English-language works that would be banned for obscenity in English-speaking countries.

" One can't get bored with sex.
But one is bored with making such
a tremendous issue about it. "

Henry Miller, 1964

Henry Miller, 1950

These included mildly pornographic popular novels, which kept the business afloat, but also works of real literary merit, such as James Joyce's *Haveth Childers Everywhere* (1930).

In 1934, Kahane published *Tropic of Cancer*. Miller gave copies of the novel to major literary figures and received favorable responses from many, including T. S. Eliot in the UK and John Dos Passos in the US. However, the US Customs Service banned imports of *Tropic of Cancer* because of its explicit sexual content, as did the British authorities. Kahane published two more works by Miller, *Black Spring* (1936) and *Tropic of Capricorn* (1939), which met the same fate. With the outbreak of World War II, Miller returned to the US.

Only at the end of the 1950s did the climate change, thanks to US publisher Barney Rosset of the Grove Press. In 1959, Rosset mounted a successful legal challenge to the ban of D. H. Lawrence's *Lady Chatterley's Lover* (see page 52), establishing the principle of "redeeming social or literary value" to counter charges of obscenity.

After his success with *Lady Chatterley's Lover,* Rosset turned his attention to *Tropic of Cancer*. In June 1961, the US Post Office seized some Obelisk Press copies but backed down when the federal authorities concluded that its ban could not be sustained. However, it could still be challenged at local and state levels, and bans in Chicago, Massachusetts, and Florida ensued, though all were overturned. At the same time, London publisher John Calder, encouraged by Grove Press's example, issued *Tropic of Cancer* in Britain, selling 40,000 copies in the first day. Miller was finally a best-selling author.

Anaïs Nin

Miller's lover and friend Anaïs Nin wrote the last book Jack Kahane published before his death. *The Winter of Artifice* (1939) consists of three sexually explicit novellas, the first based on Nin's relationship with Miller and his second wife, June. After publishing a shortened version of the work in 1942, Nin claimed that the original book had been banned by the US Postal Service. She remained little known until the publication of the first volume of her diaries in 1966.

Mephisto

Klaus Mann

1936

Banned in both Nazi Germany and, later, West Germany, Klaus Mann's novel *Mephisto* tells the story of a German actor, Hendrik Höfgen, who, having moved in leftist circles in the 1920s, consorts with leading Nazis after they come to power. Like Faust of German legend, who sells his soul to the devil's servant Mephistopheles, Höfgen sells his integrity for power and status in the Third Reich.

The novel was published in Amsterdam, where Klaus Mann lived in exile (his family, including his father, the novelist Thomas Mann, had been stripped of German citizenship for their anti-fascist stands). *Mephisto* was more than an anti-Nazi satire, however; it had a personal dimension. Höfgen was modeled on the actor Gustaf Gründgens, whom Nazi Hermann Göring appointed Director of the Berlin State Theatre after seeing him play Mephistopheles in Goethe's *Faust*. In addition, Gründgens and Mann had reputedly once been lovers.

After the war, Gründgens remained popular in West Germany, and Mann's German publisher did not wish to antagonize him by publishing *Mephisto*. In 1949, Mann died by suicide, and in 1963, Gründgens also killed himself. The following year, a Munich publisher proposed publishing *Mephisto*, but Gründgens's lover objected. After seven years of legal proceedings, the German supreme court ruled that Gründgens's posthumous reputation was more important than freedom from censorship.

Eventually, in 1981, another publisher defied the ban and brought out a paperback edition of *Mephisto*. No legal action followed. That same year, Hungarian director István Szabó's film *Mephisto*, based on the novel, won an Oscar for Best Foreign Language Film.

Gone With the Wind

Margaret Mitchell

1936

A n instant best-seller, *Gone with the Wind* tells the story of Scarlett O'Hara, the pampered daughter of a plantation family whose great wealth and lavish lifestyle are built on the labor of enslaved people. Beginning in the run-up to the Civil War (1861–1865), it paints a rose-tinted picture of antebellum life. It does not show the evils of slavery or discuss the aims of the North—the preservation of the Union and, eventually, the abolition of slavery.

Some Black Americans objected to the book from the start. When David O. Selznick bought the film rights shortly after the book's publication, a group of Black Americans in Pittsburgh told him, "We consider this work to be a glorification of the old rotten system of slavery, propaganda for race-hatreds and bigotry, and incitement of lynching." The film's glorification of white supremacy appealed to Adolf Hitler, though the Nazis went on to ban the book because subjugated people in Nazi-occupied Europe identified with the embattled South.

In the US, some readers objected to the book's coarse language, the positive depiction of a sex worker, and thrice-married Scarlett's immorality. Today, objections center on the use of the N-word and the book's warped view of American history. It was banned in Anaheim, California, in 1978, and challenged in Waukegan, Illinois, in 1984. The film, and so the book, came under the spotlight again in 2020, when John Ridley, screenwriter of *Twelve Years a Slave*, objected to the film of the novel being put on the US streaming service HBO Max without a disclaimer about its accuracy. HBO temporarily withdrew the film, later reinstating it with an introduction explaining its history and racism.

Their Eyes Were Watching God

Zora Neale Hurston

1937

Many consider Zora Neale Hurston to be one of the most influential Black American writers of the 20th century. Her second novel, *Their Eyes Were Watching God*, the story of a Southern Black woman's search for true love, is a seminal work that features on many high school and undergraduate reading lists. Structured as a third-person narrative, it is told through protagonist Janie Crawford's recollections of her life, using vernacular language and speech patterns. The spectacle of a "dust-bearing bee" sinking into a pear blossom marks the start of her journey of self-discovery.

The novel received a lukewarm reception. Hurston's peers criticized what they saw as a lack of political engagement, while some of her readers thought the novel's "Black-inflected dialect" portrayed Black people as simple-minded. Falling out of favor with readers, Hurston's work went out of print during her lifetime.

Hurston was rediscovered in the 1970s thanks to the efforts of Alice Walker, author of *The Color Purple*. Scholars now praised Hurston's ability to capture her characters through their Southern

> " Her characters ... swing like a pendulum eternally in that safe and narrow orbit in which America likes to see the Negro live: between laughter and tears. "

Richard Wright, 1937

Cover of the first edition, 1937

dialect. However, the vernacular style once again proved controversial, not least because of the novel's inclusion of racial slurs—particularly the N-word. In 1997, the parents of one student in Brentsville, Virginia, questioned the novel's inclusion on a summer reading list at Stonewall Jackson High School, citing the inappropriate language and sexual content, even though it contains very few allusions to sex. The challenge was dismissed on the grounds that the book was optional.

The Grapes of Wrath

John Steinbeck

1939

It was the best-selling American book of the year 1939, a winner of both the Pulitzer Prize and the National Book Award. It was later cited as the chief reason that its author, John Steinbeck, won the Nobel Prize for Literature in 1962. But *The Grapes of Wrath*, Steinbeck's most heartfelt and uncompromising work, divided America.

The book's admirers found the saga of the Joad family's odyssey from the Oklahoma "Dust Bowl," where they have been forced off their land by drought and bank foreclosures, to the delusory Promised Land of California to be the prototype American Tragedy and the great social justice novel of its day. Many a tear sprang at Tom Joad's famous farewell to Ma: "Wherever they's a fight so hungry people can eat, I'll be there." The novel's detractors, on the other hand, saw Steinbeck as a propagandist, casting the banks, land companies, and orchard owners as capitalist villains and calling for the people to mount a social revolution.

Decade after decade, *The Grapes of Wrath* was banned in one school district after another—from Missouri to California, and South Carolina to New York State—often for its coarse language or perceived attacks on capitalism or religion. It was banned outside the US, too, in Ireland in 1953, and in Turkey in 1973. Yet such attempts at censorship have not slowed the novel's momentum. In an age of migration and climate crisis, *The Grapes of Wrath* remains relevant today. Along with Steinbeck's *Of Mice and Men*, it is one of the most frequently taught books in American high schools and colleges, and widely read in other countries. True to his promise, Tom Joad has never gone away.

Cover of the 1939 edition

" It was publicly banned and burned by citizens, it was debated on national radio; but above all, it was read. "

Peter Lisca, 1958

The Postwar Years

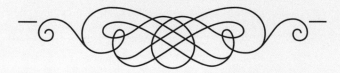

Black Boy

Richard Wright

1945

A memoir documenting Black author Richard Wright's experiences of racism, poverty, and domestic violence, *Black Boy* has been repeatedly banned or restricted in US schools. Objections have centered on its graphic sexual content, strong language, and the very racialized violence the author seeks to expose as he describes his childhood in Mississippi, Arkansas, and Tennessee before moving to Chicago, becoming a writer, and joining the Communist Party.

> **"** I would hurl words into this darkness and wait for an echo. **"**

Richard Wright, 1945

In the 1970s, parental objections to the book led to its temporary removal from classrooms in Michigan, Louisiana, Tennessee, and New York. In New York, access to the book was restricted by the need for parental approval in the Island Trees New York school district until the US Supreme Court ruled in *Board of Education v. Pico* that a school could not limit access to books because of the ideas expressed in them.

In 1997, a minister in Jacksonville, Florida, sought the book's removal from schools, saying that it might spark "hard feelings" between students of different races. Ten years later, the Livingston Organization for Values in Education accused Howell Public High Schools in Livingston County, Michigan, of distributing "sexually explicit materials" to minors by making *Black Boy* available. The prosecutor found that the passages illustrated larger literary, artistic, or political messages that did not violate criminal laws, and the case was dropped.

The Diary of a Young Girl

Anne Frank

1947

Anne Frank was a young Jewish girl who kept a diary while hiding from the Nazis in Amsterdam during World War II. She and her family spent two years in the secret annex of a house with another Jewish family and a man who was a friend of her father. Discovered and arrested in August 1944, they were sent to concentration camps where all but Anne's father, Otto, died of disease or were killed.

Discovered and published by Otto after the war, the diary is a vital eyewitness account of the Holocaust and widely used to teach young people about the war. Yet this important book, which has been translated into more than 70 languages, has been banned multiple times, usually because of its references to puberty and Anne's burgeoning sexuality. In 1983, the diary was also challenged by the State Textbook Committee in Alabama for being "too depressing."

A number of US schools have removed passages considered inappropriate for children, while a German publisher, in 1950, omitted sections deemed offensive to German readers. In 2009, a school in Lebanon banned the diary on the grounds that it promoted Zionism.

1984

George Orwell
1949

For a few weeks in 2018, social media users in China found they could not type 1,9, 8, and 4 in that sequence. Those key strokes, it seemed, were getting perilously close to "1984"—the title of George Orwell's dystopian masterpiece.

1984 depicts a totalitarian state, where Big Brother's inescapable gaze hovers over a world in which mere thoughts can be crimes, love is forbidden, and the terrors of Room 101, where prisoners are confronted by their greatest fear, are unendurable. The central character, Winston Smith, works as a fact-changer in the Ministry of Truth, revising "every kind of literature or documentation which might conceivably hold any political or ideological significance."

Since the specter of Stalinist Russia lay behind *1984*, all totalitarian states clamped down on the novel. The Soviet Union banned it from 1950 until 1990. Misreadings also led to condemnation in less predictable places. Jackson County, Florida, for example, charged it with being "pro-communist."

> ❝ *1984* is a handbook
> for difficult times. ❞
>
> **Jean Seaton**, 2018

China dropped its ban on the novel in 1985. The censoring of any mention of *1984* on Chinese social media in 2018 was a recognition of the speed at which parallels drawn between *1984* and China could go viral. "Newspeak," the official language of Orwell's totalitarian state ("designed to diminish the range of thought") is not unlike groupthink, the phenomenon that helps stories and images go viral. Equally, Orwell's telescreens—which capture people's every movement and conversation—have similarities with today's smartphones.

George Orwell broadcasting for the BBC in 1941

The Hive

Camilo José Cela

1951

During Francisco Franco's dictatorship (1939–1975), Spanish culture was heavily censored. All literary and visual works had to be submitted for government approval. Even the censors were not exempted from scrutiny, as author Camilo José Cela, who had worked as a censor from 1943–1944, discovered when he tried to publish his novel *The Hive* (*La colmena* in Spanish).

The Hive offers a somber and damning portrait of Madrid (the "hive" of the title) after the Spanish Civil War (1936–1939), which brought Franco to power. Spanning three days in 1942, it exposes the despair and poverty in a community suffering from political repression. When Cela submitted the book to the censors in 1946, it was rejected for having scarce literary value and for attacking Spanish values.

Cela published his work in Argentina in 1951, and in Spain in 1963, but due to censorship in both countries, it is unclear how much was altered or lost. In 2014, an early, unedited manuscript was found featuring highly erotic scenes—one involving two women and another a sex worker. In 2016, 14 years after Cela's death, the Royal Spanish Academy published a new edition that contained these scenes in an appendix to commemorate the centennial of the author's birth.

Cover of the first Spanish edition of *The Hive* (*La colmena*)

> " *La colmena* is just a slice of life, a pale reflection of daily, bitter, lovable, painful reality. "

Camilo José Cela

The Catcher in the Rye

❧

J. D. Salinger

1951

Between 1961 and 1982, J. D. Salinger's *The Catcher in the Rye* was the most frequently censored book in US high schools and libraries. Written from the perspective of Holden Caulfield, a troubled 16-year-old in what appears to be a sanatorium, it describes what happened when he dropped out of his elite private school just before the Christmas vacation and spent two days drifting in New York. Among other experiences, he has an encounter with a sex worker and her pimp in a hotel room.

The impact of the novel was explosive. Its empathy for a disaffected adolescent had rarely, if ever, been seen before in fiction. *The Catcher in the Rye* soon became what it has remained—one of the most popular required texts in high schools. For many, however, it was deeply subversive. Parents objected to its sexual references and bad language, and complained that Holden Caulfield was a bad role model who undermined "family values."

In 1960, a teacher was fired from a school in Tulsa, Oklahoma, for teaching *The Catcher in the Rye* to eleventh-graders—students of Caulfield's own age. The teacher appealed and was reinstated, but the novel remained

J. D. Salinger, 1951

> " [Caulfield's] minor delinquencies seem minor indeed when contrasted with the adult delinquencies with which he is confronted. "

The New York Times, 1951

banned at the school. Objections to the book, which rumbled on throughout the US school system, were compounded when it was revealed that Mark David Chapman had a copy of the book on him when he assassinated former Beatle John Lennon in 1980. Chapman later claimed that "a large part of me is Holden Caulfield." If nothing else, the association showed how deeply the novel had penetrated the American psyche.

Fahrenheit 451

Ray Bradbury

1953

" [S]ome cubbyhole editors at Ballantine Books, fearful of contaminating the young, had, bit by bit, censored some 75 different sections from the novel. "

Ray Bradbury, 1979

In this dystopian vision of the future, a "fireman" is not a preserver but a destroyer, not one who douses the flames but rather one who sets things ablaze, principally books. The very title, *Fahrenheit 451*, refers to the temperature at which paper combusts. Books, it seems, are carriers of ideas—which are dangerous to totalitarians.

Ray Bradbury's evocative tale is of a fireman who goes renegade. Charged with burning books in a futuristic US city, Guy Montag turns his back on the anodyne television screens, which hold most people in thrall, in order to seek out those who still cherish the written word.

Fahrenheit 451 is a warning about government censorship, but this did not deter the censors. In 1987, in the most publicized of several school challenges in the US, the Bay County School Board in Panama City, Florida, swept it out of the classroom for "vulgarity." A class-action lawsuit and protests by students eventually led to its reinstatement.

Most surprisingly, in the 1960s and '70s, the book's publisher, Ballantine Books, released an expurgated edition of *Fahrenheit 451* intended for high school students.

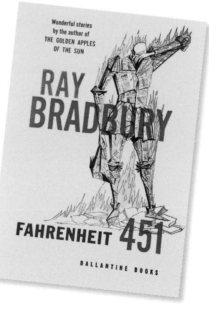

Not only were swear words removed, but characters were manipulated and some episodes were entirely recast, all without the author's knowledge. What was worse, for six years, from 1973–1979, the expurgated edition was the only version of the novel offered for sale in the US.

On learning of the expurgated edition from a friend, Bradbury demanded that it be withdrawn. In 1980, the original edition was back in print, stating in the coda: "There is more than one way to burn a book."

Cover of the first edition of *Fahrenheit 451*, 1953

The Lord of the Flies

William Golding
1954

A best seller in the 1950s and '60s, *The Lord of the Flies*, by British author William Golding, is the story of a group of schoolboys marooned by a plane crash on a desert island. The oldest, Ralph, initially takes the lead and tries to organize the group as a benign, democratic society, but he is no match for a savage undertow that emerges, represented by the dictatorial Jack, his rival. Under Jack's leadership, bloodthirsty rites emerge, and two of the boys are murdered. The group is only rescued—from itself, above all—by the arrival of a naval officer.

The book's depiction of the boys' descent into lawlessness and brutality makes for disturbing reading, which not everyone thought suitable for children, even though the book is popular assigned reading in schools. Over the decades, there have been many attempts to have it banned from schools and libraries. In 1981, for example, it was challenged in a high school in South Dakota on the grounds that it suggested humans were little better than animals. In Canada, in 1988, the Toronto Board of Education condemned its representation of the island's Indigenous inhabitants and advised schools to withdraw it.

The novel reflects racist ideologies common in the mid-1950s, and Golding clearly had in mind the children's classic *The Coral Island* (1857), by R. M. Ballantyne, in which a group of children take over a Pacific island, face down pirates and hostile locals, and claim the island for Queen Victoria. Part of Golding's intention was to question the glib expectations of human nature and society represented in such stories.

> " Promptly authority is undermined, the common spirit split. Two camps are formed, and the fatal seed of rivalry, of hatred, is sown. "

The New York Times, 1955

Lolita

Vladimir Nabokov

1955

Vladimir Nabokov's fictional case-study of Humbert Humbert, a middle-aged pedophile who describes and eventually realizes his fantasies about his 12-year-old stepdaughter, is one of the most controversial works of literature. Even while writing it, Nabokov, a Russian-born writer living in the US, knew his third English novel would be contentious—he contemplated abandoning it—and initially sought to publish the work under a pseudonym, fearing the impact the novel might have on his career as a university professor.

Publishers in the US and UK turned down *Lolita* when Nabokov submitted the novel in 1954. Eventually published in 1955 by Olympia Press, an English-language publishing house in France, it immediately faced an intense backlash. The UK prohibited imports of the novel, describing it as pornographic and "utter filth," and the French government banned it in 1956, leading to a public lawsuit between Olympia and the Administrative Tribunal in Paris. The publisher initially won the case, but lost on appeal. It was only after the novel was successfully published in French by another publisher that the ban on Olympia's English edition was lifted in France.

Outside France, *Lolita* was published in the US without restrictions in 1958, though it was banned by a number of public libraries. The novel remained banned in the UK until 1959, when the reformed Obscene Publications Act allowed literary merit to be taken into account when determining if a work should be censored. The book's publisher, Weidenfeld & Nicolson, had long wanted to publish *Lolita*, and Nigel Nicolson—an MP at the time—ruined his political career by campaigning in favor of the book, against the judgment of many fellow Conservatives.

> " Mr. Nabokov, whose English vocabulary would astound the editors of the Oxford dictionary, does not write cheap pornography. He writes highbrow pornography ... Nevertheless, *Lolita* is disgusting. "

The New York Times, 1958

Vladimir Nabokov, in 1958

Giovanni's Room

James Baldwin

1956

When James Baldwin first showed his second novel, *Giovanni's Room*, to his editors at New York publisher Knopf in 1956, their response was emphatic. They could not possibly publish the novel and they advised Baldwin to burn the manuscript. Set in Paris in the 1950s, the novel tells the story of a doomed love affair between David, a young bisexual American in Paris, and Giovanni, a beautiful Italian bartender. The relationship does not include any explicit sex scenes, yet Knopf considered it explosive.

Sexual attraction between two men was not the only controversy with the novel. Baldwin's first—and strongly autobiographical—novel *Go Tell It on the Mountain* (1953), about a young Black preacher in Harlem, was seen as an appropriate and acceptable subject for a Black writer. In *Giovanni's Room*, however, Baldwin, who had been living in France since 1948, tackled more controversial themes. Not only was his new novel set in Europe, but his protagonist was white. It was thought that this might be seen as presumptuous by some white readers while also alienating Black fans.

Knopf was afraid of a backlash if they published the novel. In fact, nuance and the ability to provoke empathy were precisely Baldwin's strengths as a novelist, and are skilfully employed in David's terrified ambivalence—caught between his love for Giovanni and his more conventional attachment to his fiancée Hella.

Baldwin's response to Knopf was furious contempt. His British publisher, Michael Joseph, made it clear that the company would publish the novel whatever the consequences. His New York agent subsequently found a smaller up-and-coming publisher, Dial Press, which published the novel in 1956.

" If Americans can mature on the level of racism, then they have to mature on the level of sexuality. "

James Baldwin, 1984

Doctor Zhivago

Boris Pasternak

1957

" Men who are not free always idealize their bondage. **"**

Doctor Zhivago

Boris Pasternak with Olga Ivinskaya (left), his inspiration for Lara, and her daughter Irina

With an epic historical sweep encompassing the final years of czarist Russia through to the revolution of 1917, the civil war, and the rise of the dictator Stalin, Boris Pasternak's novel, *Doctor Zhivago*, is one of the outstanding works of Russian literature. Its very power as a novel, however, made it a threat to the Soviet authorities.

Previously best known for his poetry, Pasternak completed *Zhivago* at the end of 1955. It was his only novel, and he had been working on it for decades. It tells the story of the doctor–poet Yuri Zhivago, as he struggles to preserve his personal integrity amid the upheaval of war and revolution, torn between his love for his wife and family and his passion for his soulmate, the beautiful nurse Lara. While not directly autobiographical, the novel reflects Pasternak's own responses to the extraordinary slice of history he had lived through.

In 1956, Pasternak submitted *Zhivago* to the literary magazine, *Novy Mir*. He was optimistic that it might be accepted, but, if need be, he was prepared to omit passages that might be considered offensive.

The months passed, and no word came from *Novy Mir*. In the meantime, in May, Pasternak was approached by a representative of Giangiacomo Feltrinelli, a Milan-based publisher. News of Pasternak's novel had reached the West and Feltrinelli wished to secure translation rights. Somewhat impulsively, Pasternak handed over a typescript.

Unbeknown to Pasternak, his novel was provoking alarm waves at the highest levels of the Soviet state. A report submitted to the Central Committee Presidium referred to it as a "heinous calumny" of the achievements of the Bolshevik Revolution of 1917. In September 1956, the editors of *Novy Mir* wrote to decline the novel. They attacked its focus on a single (bourgeois) individual, Yuri Zhivago, which, they claimed, demeaned the struggle to create a new collectivist order.

Publication in the West started to look like Pasternak's best option. Although he seems not to have been aware of it, his contract with Feltrinelli gave the Italian publisher control of all foreign rights. Amid huge publicity, *Doctor Zhivago* appeared for the first time, in Italian, in November 1957, its first print run of 6,000 selling out within a day. English, French, and other translations followed, along with a Russian edition in the Netherlands (funded, it is now known, by the CIA, who with Britain's MI6 soon spotted the novel's propaganda value).

The novel's success in the West increased hostility toward it in Russia. The Soviet authorities saw the fanfare surrounding *Zhivago* in a purely political light, as an insult to their system. It was not until 1988, after Mikhail Gorbachev's rise to power, that *Zhivago* was published for the first time in Russia—by *Novy Mir*.

Nobel no more

When, on October 23, 1958, the Swedish Academy announced Pasternak as the winner of that year's Nobel Prize for Literature, the Soviet authorities reacted with fury. A Writers' Union official visited Pasternak, demanding that he reject the prize, which the authorities saw as an anti-Soviet political ploy. When Pasternak refused to comply, the Soviet authorities launched a vitriolic press campaign against him, and on the October 27, he was expelled from the Writers' Union. Two days later, a near-suicidal Pasternak sent a telegram to the Swedes, renouncing his previous acceptance of "this unmerited prize."

Cover for the 1958 English edition of *Doctor Zhivago*

❝ We feel that *Dr. Zhivago* is an excellent springboard for conversations with Soviets on the general theme of Communism versus freedom of expression. ❞

CIA memo, 1959

Borstal Boy

Brendan Behan

1958

The Irish writer Brendan Behan's novel *Borstal Boy* is a surprisingly affectionate account of life in a borstal, a British juvenile detention center, in the mid-20th century. The novel depicts an environment where violence and the harshness of the regime are unable to obliterate genuine solidarity and kindness among the inmates, despite radical differences in their backgrounds and upbringing.

Borstal Boy is based closely on Behan's own experiences. Born into a strongly republican family in Dublin in 1923, he joined the Irish Republican Army (IRA) at the age of 16. Shortly afterward, he was arrested by the British authorities in Liverpool, on a self-appointed mission to set off a bomb in the docks, and sentenced to three years in a borstal. On his release in 1941, Behan returned to Dublin where his

> " The first duty of a writer is to let his country down. "

Brendan Behan

Brendan Behan, c. 1955

IRA activism led to his imprisonment in an Irish jail. Released in 1946, and rejecting republican violence, he embarked on a new life as a writer. His 1954 play, *The Quare Fellow*—set in a prison—was a hit in Dublin and London's West End. Another play, *The Hostage*, followed in 1958, along with *Borstal Boy*, published in London by Hutchinson.

In December 1958, Hutchinson sent copies of *Borstal Boy* to Dublin for the Christmas market. The consignment was seized by customs officers and promptly banned by the Irish Censorship of Publications Board. The board was not obliged to give its reasons. Probable factors include critical allusions to both Irish republicanism and the Catholic church, the use of "bad" language, and suggestions of homosexual activity among the boys. The book was also censored in Australia and New Zealand. Behan marked the Irish ban by composing a ditty about joining the ranks of "the best banned in the land."

Behan, bedeviled by alcoholism and diabetes, died in 1964, aged 41. Three years later, *Borstal Boy* was adapted as a stage play, which won a Tony Award on Broadway in 1970, the year that the Irish ban on the novel lapsed. The novel was made into a film in 2000.

Things Fall Apart

Chinua Achebe
1958

First published in 1958, in the final years of British rule in Nigeria, Chinua Achebe's *Things Fall Apart* details the detrimental effects of colonialism on Okonkwo, the Igbo leader of a fictional Nigerian village. Over the course of the novel, the structure of Igbo society disintegrates as Christianity replaces traditional culture.

Achebe said he was reclaiming his Igbo identity in the novel, but many Nigerians interpreted the novel's conclusion—Okonkwo dies by suicide to avoid punishment from the colonizers—as Achebe's belief in the collapse of Igbo culture. At the same time, the novel's criticism of colonialism caused a stir in some former colonies. Malaysia—a British colony until 1957—reportedly imposed an outright ban on the novel.

Things Fall Apart appears on high school and university reading lists around the world, for both its literary and political importance, but it remains controversial. In 2012, Nigerian actor Femi Robinson called (unsuccessfully) for the Nigerian government to ban it from schools, claiming that Achebe had been "selling hate and disunity." In 2012, complaints that his work could be "politically, racially, or socially offensive" were filed at Centennial High School in Burleson, Texas, in an unsuccessful attempt to ban the novel. Others have argued that its themes need careful handling. In 2014, Oberlin College in Ohio listed the novel as one that should come with a content warning, as it could traumatize students who had experienced its themes first-hand. While some academics view content warnings as a form of censorship, others argue that they can widen access by allowing readers to approach a text when they are mentally prepared.

Naked Lunch

William S. Burroughs

1959

American writer William S. Burroughs's *Naked Lunch* would eventually become a counterculture classic, but when it was published at the end of the 1950s, this hallucinatory account of drug addiction provoked outrage in the US.

Written in Tangier, Morocco (the seedy "interzone" in which the book is partly set) in the late 1950s, *Naked Lunch* was published in Paris in 1959. Apart from being a tale about drug use, it is laced with profanities and includes depictions of gay sex. Copies that reached US shores were labeled as obscene and confiscated by customs agents.

When a US edition was published in 1962, it was banned, leading to courtroom showdowns in Boston and Los Angeles. Even though poet Allen Ginsberg and novelist Norman Mailer testified to the book's literary merits, the judges were dubious. In Los Angeles, the bench ruled that it was not obscene, though the judge did find it appalling. In Boston, the case went all the way to the Massachusetts Supreme Court, which relied on the decision of a 1966 US Supreme Court to curtail the power of any governing body to ban or regulate artistic content. The Massachusetts Supreme Court dismissed the obscenity charges on *Naked Lunch*—ending the last literary censorship battle on US soil.

A Raisin in the Sun

Lorraine Hansberry

1959

" I can't imagine a contemporary writer any place in the world today who isn't in conflict with his world. "

Lorraine Hansberry

Lorraine Hansberry in her New York apartment, 1959

When Lorraine Hansberry's play *A Raisin in the Sun* opened on Broadway in 1959 it was a monumental success both critically and commercially, running for 530 performances and winning the New York Drama Critics' Circle award for Best American Play. Set in an apartment on Chicago's South Side, the play presents a Black American family standing up against racism and segregation.

The play's text has been repeatedly challenged in schools, for raising topics such as racial conflict, feminism, and abortion. In 1995, the play fell foul of New Hampshire's Merrimack School Board's Prohibition of Alternative Lifestyle Instruction policy, banning the teaching of materials that "encouraged" same-sex relationships or were written by LGBTQ+ writers. Although Hansberry did not come out as a lesbian, her affiliation with the Daughters of Bilitis—a lesbian organization—and her romantic relationships with women were public knowledge. As a result, *A Raisin in the Sun* was listed as a prohibited text, unleashing a huge backlash. The ban was eventually dropped in 1996, when protesters filed a federal lawsuit against the school board.

To Kill a Mockingbird

Harper Lee

1960

Harper Lee's Pulitzer Prize–winning novel *To Kill A Mockingbird* is about the trial of a black man, Tom Robinson, who has been falsely accused of raping a white woman in a small town in Alabama in the 1930s. The protagonist, Scout Finch, is a young girl whose father is the lawyer for the defendant. As the story develops, Scout learns about inequality and racism. Toward the end, Robinson is found guilty by the racist jury and shot while trying to escape from custody.

Since it is told from a child's perspective, *To Kill A Mockingbird* is often viewed as a children's book, and it is frequently used to teach young people about American history, segregation, and racism. However, while the novel is true to the place and times in which it is set, there are questions about how relevant it is today. There are frequent calls, sometimes successful, for its removal from the curriculum for a variety of reasons: the sexual assault; the implication that women lie about being raped; the racist language, including use of the N-word; and its treatment of racism. In recent years, the book has been criticized for its "white savior" complex, as the plot revolves around a white lawyer helping a Black man. This reason was cited by an Edinburgh school that removed it from its curriculum in 2021. Some critics argue that the book, which is by a white author, should be removed in order to make space for more works by Black writers.

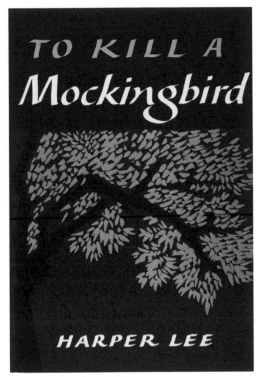

Cover of the first edition, 1960

❝ You never really understand a person until you consider things from his point of view ... Until you climb inside of his skin and walk around in it. ❞

Harper Lee, in *To Kill a Mockingbird*

Catch-22

Joseph Heller

1961

Soon after its publication, Joseph Heller's *Catch-22* was being hailed as the Great American Antiwar Novel. Its protagonist, Captain John Yossarian, a B-25 bombardier during World War II, is a comic antihero primarily concerned with his own survival. The sheer terror of each mission flown over enemy skies is amplified by group commander Colonel Cathcart always increasing the number of missions that have to be completed before pilots can be discharged. This creates a comi-tragic theater of the absurd epitomized by the "catch-22" of the title: you cannot plead insanity as a means of getting discharged because wanting to be discharged is the sanest act of all.

Catch-22 was popular with college students during the antiauthoritarian 1960s and early '70s when the Vietnam War divided public opinion around the globe. In the US, some supporters of the war considered the book to be a dangerous influence, although attempts to have it removed from libraries mainly centered on offensive language.

A ban of the novel in Strongsville, Ohio, in 1972, led to a celebrated court case four years later—*Minarcini v. Strongsville City School District*. Citing the First Amendment, the Sixth US Court of Appeals overturned a lower court ruling supporting a ban, stating that school boards could not simply winnow out books they disliked from school libraries, which were "an important privilege ... not subject to being withdrawn by succeeding school boards." Nonetheless, *Catch-22* continues to be challenged. In 2020, Mat-Su Borough School District in Alaska, attempted (unsuccessfully) to have it removed from schools, along with several other works, citing racism and misogyny.

“ The characters speak with typical ‘military men’ misogyny and racist attitudes of the time. There are scenes of violence both hand-to-hand and with guns, and violence against women. ”

Mat-Su Borough School District, Alaska, 2019

A Clockwork Orange

Anthony Burgess

1962

<blockquote>
" I begin to accept that, as a novelist,
I belong to the ranks of the menacing. "

Anthony Burgess, 1993
</blockquote>

A poster from the film of the book

Anthony Burgess's terrifying dystopian novel *A Clockwork Orange* portrays a world of extreme violence, police brutality, and state control. Alex, the narrator and main character, lives for violence and the graphic scenes of beatings and rape are seen from his point of view. The moral question at the heart of the novel is revealed when, to get out of jail, Alex volunteers for an experimental program that will turn him from a violent thug into a model citizen. The book asks whether goodness without free will is goodness at all.

In 1971, Stanley Kubrick's film of the novel came out in the US. Banned for its extreme violence in parts of the US, and by a number of councils in Britain when it was released there, the film suddenly drew attention to the novel. There were unsuccessful attempts to remove it from some US libraries, and a bookseller in Utah was briefly arrested for selling it. Ironically, the most effective ban of the film was by Kubrick, who came to believe that it inspired violence and took it out of circulation in the UK in 1973. The film was not rereleased until 2019.

One Flew Over the Cuckoo's Nest

Ken Kesey
1962

Described by *The New York Times* as a "glittering parable of good and evil," Ken Kesey's novel *One Flew Over the Cuckoo's Nest* has a long history of censorship. Set in a psychiatric hospital in Oregon in the 1950s, it describes what happens when Randle McMurphy—a criminal feigning insanity to avoid prison—arrives on the ward, overturning the rules laid down by the terrifying Nurse Ratched. His influence is joyfully subversive, but it also has some devastating consequences.

Between 1971 and 1986, *One Flew Over the Cuckoo's Nest* was challenged by parents and school boards in at least nine US states. To its opponents, its scenes of violence, sex, torture, suicide, and murder, as well as repeated racial slurs directed at Black patients, overshadow its value in exploring issues such as mental ill-health and the dangers of social conformity. In 1974, the novel, along with other titles, was removed from school libraries in Strongsville, Ohio, after five parents successfully sued the school board, calling the novel "pornographic" and claiming it would corrupt readers through its glorification of criminal activity. (The verdict was overturned on appeal two years later.) In 1975, the districts of Randolph, New York, and Alton, Oklahoma, also removed the novel from public school libraries; three years later, Freemont High School in St. Anthony, Idaho, dismissed a teacher who assigned the text.

Some schools rejected pressures to censor the book. In 1982 and 1986, schools in New Hampshire and Washington refused to remove it from reading lists, as did the Placentia-Yorba Linda Unified School District in California, in 2000.

> " I don't want to put these kind
> of images in children's minds. "

Parent, Placentia-Yorba Linda Unified School District, 2000

Poster for the 1975 movie of the novel

The Late 20th Century

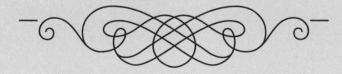

The Autobiography of Malcolm X

—◇—

Malcolm X & Alex Haley

1965

In 1952, Malcolm Little walked out of prison and put a life of crime behind him. He discarded the surname Little, which he saw as a name imposed on his family by white enslavers, for Malcolm X, the "X" representing his lost African ancestry, and became a radical Black activist. A new convert to the Nation of Islam, an offshoot of the Black Muslim movement, he quickly became a messiah-like figure to his followers, advocating Black nationalism and characterizing white people's racial terrorism as irredeemable. However, after breaking with the Nation of Islam in 1964, he moderated his stance.

On February 21, 1965, Malcolm X was assassinated by former associates in the Nation of Islam. Eight months later, *The Autobiography of Malcolm X* was published, based on audio-taped interviews he had given to Black writer Alex Haley, later famous as the author of *Roots*. The book was highly praised and roundly condemned in equal measure. While sales climbed into the millions, critics denounced the book's "anti-white statements" and condemned its descriptions of criminal activity as a "how-to" manual for offenders.

Many schools and libraries across the US simply excluded *The Autobiography of Malcolm X* when it first came out. In recent years, its inclusion on school reading lists has been repeatedly challenged, and it is now one of the top-ten most banned volumes on Black history topics in the country. In 2014, teachers at a public school in Queens, New York, even told fourth-graders that Malcolm X was so "violent" and "bad" that they could not write about him for Black History Month.

Malcolm X in New York City, 1964

" Let sincere whites
go and teach nonviolence
to white people. "

Malcolm X, 1965

In Cold Blood

Truman Capote

1965

When American author Truman Capote published *In Cold Blood* in 1966, he claimed to have invented a new literary genre: the "nonfiction novel." Originally serialized in *The New Yorker* in four installments in the year prior to publication, the novel offered a fictionalized account of the Clutter family murders, which took place in Kansas in 1959. After cutting Herbert Clutter's throat and shooting him, the perpetrators murdered his wife and two teenage children in order to eliminate witnesses. Imagining the thoughts and final moments of the victims, as well as the movements of the killers, Capote painted a vivid picture of the lives lost and the minds of the people who ended them.

True crime has long fascinated the general public: the genre now spans literature, TV, movies, and radio. The teaching of *In Cold Blood* in US schools, however, has disturbed some parents, who question the impact reading about violent real-life events could have upon young people. In 2011, the Glendale Unified School District in California tried to stop the book from being studied by its 16–17-year-old students because of its violence. The teacher who wished to add the novel to the district's English curriculum defended its literary merit, also stating that Capote's account allowed for class discussions on many important topics, including the American judicial system. She also highlighted the advanced level of the class itself, saying the novel was only appropriate for this mature group. Although school officials were divided by the case, the school board ultimately chose to add *In Cold Blood* to the course reading list.

> **" I think 'chilling' is far too benign a word to use. "**
>
> **Mary Boger, Glendale Unified school board**, 2011

A window display in New York City publicizes *In Cold Blood* in 1959

I Know Why The Caged Bird Sings

Maya Angelou

1969

" The fact that the adult American Negro female emerges a formidable character is often met with amazement, distaste, and even belligerence. "

Maya Angelou

The most celebrated of Maya Angelou's seven autobiographies, *I Know Why the Caged Bird Sings* is also her most controversial. Published in 1969, it chronicles Angelou's childhood and early adolescence, much of it in America's segregated South in the 1930s and '40s. Brutally honest, it reveals a childhood filled with horrifying abuse at the hands of her divorced mother and her partners. A survivor of molestation, rape, and even attempted murder, Angelou faced her struggles while writing down the events, saying "I stayed half drunk in the afternoon and cried all night." After the murder of the man who raped her when she was eight years old, Angelou blamed herself for having told her brother the name of her rapist and stopped speaking for five years.

The memoir was lauded by book critics. The review in *The Washington Post* said: "There isn't any easy, which is to say false, line in the book." After being named one of the Best Books for Young Adults by the American Library Association in 1970, *Caged Bird* started to appear on school curricula. Parents soon began complaining about Angelou's candid discussion of the trauma she suffered as a child, and it became one of the most frequently challenged books in US schools. Most of the objections revolved around Angelou's description of her rape, which some parents deemed perverse and pornographic. In 1994, parents in Castle Rock, Colorado, claimed that the book presented "a lurid tale of sexual perversion." The following year, parents in Volusia County, Florida, requested that the memoir be removed from reading lists, claiming that it "promotes cohabitation and rape."

In addition to these "gross evils"—as described by one parent in Southlake, Texas, in 1995—concerns were raised about "immoral" scenes from Angelou's adolescence. The book's ending, when the 17-year-old Angelou gives birth to her only child with no intention of getting married, prompted some parents in Austin, Texas, to claim that the text "promoted" premarital sex. In 1995, complaints that the memoir lacked "traditional values" led to its removal from classrooms in Arizona's Gilbert Unified School District.

Objections to the author's portrayal of the white people she encountered in her grandmother's general store were also raised by some groups of white parents. In 1983, the Alabama State Textbook Committee received internal complaints from members who claimed the work promoted "bitterness and hatred against whites." The alleged anti-white tone of *Caged Bird* led to it being temporarily removed from Maryland's Anne Arundel County's school curriculum, though it was eventually returned to classrooms.

Responses to the litany of complaints have varied over the years. Many school boards reject challenges, citing the memoir's literary merit. Others have conceded that the novel contains difficult subjects that may not be appropriate for younger students. In 2009, Ocean View School District in California, for example, restricted pupils' access to copies in the school library by requiring parental permission.

Other schools have sought compromises with parents. In 2006, when Fond du Lac High School in Wisconsin, faced calls for removing the memoir from the second year of an advanced placement English class, they formed a review committee to assess the situation. In the end, they agreed to notify parents of the texts being taught, so they

A full life

Maya Angelou once said, "I love to see a young girl go out and grab life by the lapels." After *Caged Bird*, she went on to write six more volumes of autobiography, describing her life between her son's birth and the point at which she sat down to write *Caged Bird* at the age of 40. During this time she worked as a singer, dancer, cook, and a journalist; campaigned for civil rights; and lived in Egypt and Ghana. She went on to write 10 highly acclaimed volumes of poetry, movie scripts, and plays, and to act. In 1993, she was invited to write and deliver a poem, "On the pulse of the morning," for President Clinton's inauguration ceremony.

Maya Angelou in 1978

> " Let me tell so much truth, I want
> to tell the truth in my work.
> The truth will lead me to all. "

Maya Angelou, 2013

could grant or refuse permission. In 2007, schools in Manheim Township, Pennsylvania, agreed to teach *Caged Bird* to ninth-grade (14–15-year-old) English students late in the school year, giving them time to mature before tackling the work.

In 2009, Angelou publicly addressed the attempted censorship of her work, saying "many times my books are banned by people who never read two sentences."

Slaughterhouse–Five

<figure>◇</figure>

Kurt Vonnegut
1969

Kurt Vonnegut fought in World War II and survived the 1945 firebombing of Dresden, Germany, which killed more than 25,000 people. There were ethical concerns about the bombing and some critics consider it a war crime, as it targeted civilians. During the attack, Vonnegut, a prisoner of war, was in a deep basement under the slaughterhouse where he was being held. When he emerged, he found a lunar landscape where even the stones were hot and everybody was dead. *Slaughterhouse-Five* is his response to what he encountered.

The book travels back and forth in time from the present, in which Vonnegut grapples with how to write about his experiences, to the past, in which the main character, Billy Pilgrim, is a prisoner of war in Dresden, and to the future, when Billy is kidnapped by aliens and taken to live on the planet Tralfamadore, where he comes to understand the transitory nature of life and the absurdity of war.

Slaughterhouse-Five was frequently banned for obscenity and violence, and for being unpatriotic because of its negative depiction of war, but in Drake, North Dakota in 1973 the book was burned. Vonnegut wrote to the school board, saying, "Books are sacred to free men for very good reasons, and wars have been fought against nations which hate books and burn them." He went on to say, "If you are an American, you must allow all ideas to circulate freely in your community, not merely your own." After the teacher who had taught *Slaughterhouse-Five* successfully sued the school board, with the help of the American Civil Liberties Union (ACLU), the book was reinstated.

Are You There, God? It's Me, Margaret

Judy Blume

1970

Judy Blume wrote this coming-of-age novel from the heart. The main character, 12-year-old Margaret, whose Jewish father and Christian mother want her to choose her religion herself when she is older, speaks directly to God about her everyday problems. Echoing Blume's own childhood worries, Margaret agonizes over when she will get breasts, and her period, and has a growing interest in boys.

The book explores these important topics gently and sensitively, yet it has been the subject of bans and challenges from the moment the author gave a copy of the first edition to her children's elementary school, only to have it quietly sidelined by the male principal as inappropriate. The book has been on the American Library Association's list of challenged books for most of the past 50 years, mainly because of its references to sexuality. In addition to school libraries that require parental permission before allowing children to check out the book, some bookstores shelve it with teen fiction, effectively putting it out of reach of the audience who needs it most—preteen girls.

Black Voices from Prison

Etheridge Knight

1970

In 1999, a prisoner in Texas requested a copy of US poet Etheridge Knight's *Black Voices from Prison*, an anthology of writings and poems by and about Black prisoners. The request was denied, prison authorities explained, because of its "racial content," specifically citing pages 30 and 47. The inmate appealed and lost, which led to the book being banned from the whole of the Texas prison system. At that time, Hitler's *Mein Kampf* (see page 50) was freely available.

In the view of the prison authorities, what made *Black Voices from Prison* more dangerous than Hitler's guide to building a totalitarian state was its frank discussion about race. On page 30, prisoner David Flournoy confesses to robbing and beating white men seeking women in Black neighborhoods, even as he "was saying no, no" to himself. Flournoy compares his struggles in America's racial caste system to being "caught in the cross-currents of two rivers meeting." On page 47, Clarence Harris describes dropping out of school and taking to the streets, rather than "trying to be white" in a culture that was like a garrote around his life.

The heart of the book is Knight's own portrait, in poetry and prose, of the "Prison America" and of the Indiana State Prison in which the other authors and Knight himself served their time. Knight's writings offer a guide to freeing the incarcerated mind but make no bones about the risks—epitomized by Hard Rock, the ultimately lobotomized inmate in a Knight poem, who "did things/We dreamed of doing but could not bring ourselves to do."

" I died in 1960 from a prison sentence and poetry brought me back to life. "

Etheridge Knight

Maurice

E. M. Forster

1971

Although British author E. M. Forster wrote *Maurice* in 1913–1914, it was not published until 1971. Forster believed that its homosexual theme rendered publication impossible without criminal sanctions—sex acts between men were illegal in England until 1967. He dedicated the manuscript "To a happier year," when a book like *Maurice* could be published, and attached a note saying that publication should only happen posthumously. After his death in 1970, the book was inherited by the gay writer Christopher Isherwood, who published it with Hodder Arnold.

The novel was inspired by a physical sensation that occurred when George Merrill, the lover and live-in partner of the writer Edward Carpenter, touched Forster on his lower back. This touch liberated Forster, enabling him to produce a novel about same-sex desire in

> **❝** I was determined that in fiction anyway two men should fall in love and remain in it for ever and ever. **❞**
>
> **E. M. Forster**, 1960

Image on the cover of the first paperback
edition, published by Penguin, 1972

which its protagonists are recognizable as emotional beings with the
capacity for love. Forster refused to go down the socially acceptable
route of having his characters' story end in misery or suicide, and the
two male characters find an enduring love together.

The novel was poorly received by critics and was often ignored in
assessments of Forster's work, but as same-sex relationships became
more acceptable in many parts of the world, *Maurice* acquired new
readers who viewed it as pioneering. Nonetheless, in 1995, a school
board in New Ipswich, New Hampshire, banned it as inappropriate for
high school students and a teacher lost her job as a result. The teacher
fought her dismissal and was reinstated the following year.

The Gulag Archipelago

Aleksandr Solzhenitsyn
1973

A single book has never done so much to undermine a world power. Aleksandr Solzhenitsyn's *The Gulag Archipelago* attacked the government of the Soviet Union head-on by attempting to tell the long story of the Gulag, the country's vast but well-concealed network of prison camps. For years, the unpublished manuscripts, written between 1958 and 1968, circulated in secret. Readers were constantly fearful of being discovered with the forbidden document, but the book's public steadily grew.

The Gulag Archipelago was finally published in France in 1973. The world was ready to listen: three years earlier Solzhenitsyn had won the Nobel Prize for Literature. Here was a serious and angry writer who had been sentenced to eight years of hard labor in the camps simply for making a veiled reference to Stalin in a letter to a friend.

Filling three volumes and nearly 2,000 pages, the work came as a shock both to Soviet citizens and to readers abroad. The book told detailed first-hand stories of interrogations, torture, corrupt camp officials, starvation, and unmarked graves. The Kremlin lashed out in fury. Solzhenitsyn was stripped of his citizenship, his archive was stolen, and he was exiled in 1974. Only after the collapse of the Soviet Union in 1991 was the book finally published in Russia. Since then, it has become required reading in many of the country's schools.

Jenny Lives with Eric and Martin

Susanne Bösche

1981

First published in Denmark, Danish author Suzanne Bösche's *Jenny Lives with Eric and Martin* is a black-and-white picture book about a five-year-old girl being raised by two fathers. Bösche wrote the book to give children a window onto families that were different from the heterosexual norm. Each chapter shows Jenny, Eric, and Martin doing everyday things, such as going to the laundromat, playing a board game together, and making up after an argument.

When the book was published in the UK in 1983, it was viewed by many politicians as "homosexual propaganda." The press stoked the uproar by reporting that it had been made available to children in school libraries—it had not (a copy had merely been given to a teachers' center to educate teachers about gay parents). Government spokespersons appeared on radio and television to argue that the book encouraged young people to accept gay relationships or even to become gay themselves.

The negative publicity probably contributed to the passing of Section 28 of the Local Government Act in 1988, which stated that local authorities could not promote homosexuality or publish material that did so. This caused some LGBTQ+ support and activist groups to shut down, publishers to self-censor, and promoted a non-LGBTQ+-friendly atmosphere throughout the UK. Section 28 was eventually repealed in 2003. Since then, many books on non-heteronormative relationships have been published for children, but *Jenny Lives with Eric and Martin* was the trailblazer.

The Color Purple

Alice Walker

1982

In 1983, Alice Walker became the first Black woman author to win the Pulitzer Prize. Her award-winning novel, *The Color Purple*, is loosely based on the life of Walker's step-grandmother. Structured as a series of intensely honest letters to God and the protagonist's sister Nettie, it follows Celie, a poor black girl growing up in the American South in the early 1900s, as she endures an abusive upbringing and subsequent marriage. Despite the odds stacked against her, Celie eventually escapes her terrible circumstances to start a new life.

The novel touches on themes of racism, sexuality, and the power of friendships between women. However, it was not unanimously lauded. Some Black American men accused Walker of perpetuating the "violent black male" stereotype, at a time when the Black community was challenging its disproportionate rates of incarceration.

Between 1984 and 2013, the book was banned (often reinstated later) by various US schools and public libraries, generally for its depictions of violence, abuse, and sex between women. In 2017, the Texas Department of Criminal Justice banned it from all state prisons, citing its references to incest. At the same time, it permitted prisoners to read Hitler's *Mein Kampf* (see page 50) and books on neo-Nazism.

Nonetheless, *The Color Purple* remains one of the most beloved books in the history of American literature. It has inspired a Tony-nominated stage musical (2005) and a film directed by Steven Spielberg (1985), which was nominated for 11 Oscars and grossed over $140 million.

Alice Walker at the premier of the stage musical in 2005

" *The Color Purple* is chosen because
[it] seems so rare, but it's everywhere.
It's in the shadows of rocks, it's in the
shadows of many things. "

Alice Walker, 2020

The House of the Spirits

Isabel Allende

1982

Set in a time of political upheaval in an unnamed Latin American country, Isabel Allende's family saga *The House of the Spirits* reflects Allende's own experiences of living in Chile in the lead-up to Augusto Pinochet's military coup in 1973. In the house of the title, where much of the story unfolds, strange supernatural phenomena are part of everyday life. Like many writers in Central and South America in the 20th century, Allende uses the genre of magic realism to criticize the status quo.

Although there are reports that the novel was banned in her native country, Allende, a relative of Salvador Allende, the Marxist president who preceded Pinochet, still won Chile's Best Novel of the Year in 1983. However, *The House of the Spirits* has proved far more controversial in the US, where it has been challenged in schools for its sexual content, violence (which includes instances of rape), and defamation of the Catholic Church. Between 1994 and 2003, the novel was unsuccessfully challenged in seven different school districts.

However, in 2013, a parent in North Carolina convinced the Watauga County Board of Education to review the novel's inclusion on the curriculum after calling its attention to explicit passages. National coverage of the challenge prompted Allende herself to write to the board, equating censorship with totalitarianism. She went on to demonstrate the critical and commercial success of her novel and its value in teaching students about Latin American history, culture, and politics. After months of hearings, the board agreed to continue teaching the novel in its schools.

> " Banning of books is common in police states like Cuba or North Korea ... but I did not expect it in our democracy. "

Isabel Allende, 2013

The House on Mango Street

Sandra Cisneros

1983

A coming-of-age novel rooted in the Chicana (Mexican-American) experience, *The House on Mango Street* by Sandra Cisneros has been at the center of two campaigns defending the right of children to learn about Latin American culture in US schools. The novel follows Esperanza, a young Chicana in Chicago, where Cisneros herself was raised. In a series of vignettes, Esperanza documents her life and that of her community. Her childish innocence allows Cisneros to explore issues such as crime and violence, including sexual assault, in a subtle way.

When the St. Helens school board in Oregon banned the novel for middle-schoolers (11–13-year-olds) in 2011, citing concerns about the "social issues presented," former students calling themselves the Mango Street Army started a campaign on Facebook in support of the novel. They said that it had helped them learn about other communities and real-world issues. Following a meeting between the school board and members of the group, the ban was officially revoked.

The most controversial ban of the novel preceded the St. Helens ban and lasted seven years. In 2010, the Governor of Arizona introduced a bill prohibiting ethnic studies—any course that was designed for a specific ethnic group, or that could "advocate ethnic solidarity," or that could "promote the overthrow of the United States Government." The ban targeted a Mexican-American program (which included Cisneros' novel) in the Tucson Unified School District. Students and teachers challenged the bill for violating the right to free speech enshrined in the First Amendment, pursuing their case through to the Court of Appeals. In 2017 the bill was deemed unconstitutional.

Sandra Cisneros, 2012

" I don't think they read the books. They just eliminated the entire whole Mexican–American studies without thinking. "

Sandra Cisneros

The Bus Stop

Gao Xingjian

1983

Regarded as the first absurdist drama in China, *The Bus Stop* tells the story of eight people, a cross-section of society, waiting for a bus to a city. More than ten years go by but no bus ever stops for them. Deeply interested in and influenced by European modernism, the playwright Gao Xingjian intended the play's seven "voices" (the eighth person is silent) to form a polyphonic symphony.

Two years before premiering *The Bus Stop*, Gao had published a small book on the techniques of modern fiction that brought him to the attention of the Anti-Spiritual-Pollution Campaign, tasked with preventing decadent Western ideas from infiltrating China's art and literature. Gao's interest in modernist concepts departed from the optimistic themes of socialist realism promoted by the Chinese state.

In 1983, when *The Bus Stop* premiered in Beijing at the People's Art Theatre, it was criticized as "the most toxic play in China" by the government and was shut down after only 13 performances. Gao's work as a writer stagnated, and when, in 1987, he was invited to Germany and France, he never returned to China. In 1989, all Gao's works, including *The Bus Stop*, were withdrawn from publication in China after he announced that he was quitting the Chinese Communist Party. This came in the wake of the pro-democracy protests in Beijing's Tiananmen Square, when Chinese troops opened fire on protesters. Yet Gao never stopped writing about China. In 2000, he was awarded the Nobel Prize for Literature "for an oeuvre of universal validity, bitter insights, and linguistic ingenuity, which has opened new paths for the Chinese novel and drama."

66 In the writing of Gao Xingjian
literature is born anew from the
struggle of the individual to survive
the history of the masses. 99

The Swedish Academy, 2000

The Handmaid's Tale

Margaret Atwood

1985

> " Lucky me, I live in a democracy, so at least I'm not in jail or being tossed out of a plane. "

Margaret Atwood

When Canadian novelist Margaret Atwood first published *The Handmaid's Tale*, her dystopian masterpiece shook readers to their core. Her exploration of a world where a woman's status is dictated by her reproductive function had many people asking not if but when such a world would come about. Described by Atwood as speculative literature rather than science fiction, it was inspired by the Puritan history of the US, the Old Testament, and Iran's Islamic Revolution. In interviews about the novel, Atwood also pointed to developments such as the rise of Christian conservatism.

The Handmaid's Tale follows Offred, a handmaid living in the Republic of Gilead—formerly the US. The world has been devastated by nuclear and environmental disasters, and as a result most of the population is sterile. Described by Atwood as a "pariah caste," the handmaids are fertile women enslaved by the dictatorial regime. The property of the regime's "Commanders" (the highest-ranking men), the handmaids are ritually raped in the hope of conceiving a child. Deprived of all rights, agency, and even prevented from reading, the handmaids find solace in each other and in rumors of an underground network seeking a way to end Gilead's regime. Other women in Gilead belong to different "castes," from wives of the Commanders to "Marthas" (cooks and maids), their status indicated by the color of their clothing. Handmaids always wear red.

Now considered a modern classic, *The Handmaid's Tale* is often taught to 14–18-year-olds in schools in the US, Canada, and the UK. Parents in the US have mounted challenges on various grounds, but only a few have been successful. The primary concern has been Atwood's graphic depiction of sex. In addition to the ritual rape, Offred describes having been taken to a brothel by her Commander, despite nonreproductive sex being prohibited in Gilead. These "lurid passages" have led to multiple petitions to ban the novel in schools.

The Handmaid's Tale, published by Vintage

There have also been allegations that the novel is offensive to Christians. The totalitarian regime of Gilead draws on Biblical references—the notion of a handmaid is taken from the Book of Genesis—and the names of characters and places are derived from the Bible. One Texas mother was successful, albeit temporarily, in getting the novel banned for being offensive to Christians. In 2006, she complained about it to the Judson School District in San Antonio, Texas, claiming she had a responsibility to the country and the community to speak up for the values that strengthen society. Before its removal, *The Handmaid's Tale* had been taught for 10 years in Judson. Eventually, the board of trustees vetoed the ban and returned the book to classrooms.

In recent years, *The Handmaid's Tale* has been claimed as a symbol of resistance. Its sales rocketed following the election of Donald Trump in 2016, along with sales of other dystopian texts, such as George Orwell's *1984* (see pages 78–79). Its popularity also surged with the release of a TV adaptation in 2017, after which the striking clothing worn by the handmaids became an international symbol of female protest, and then again with publication of Atwood's sequel, *The Testaments*, in 2019. These developments have fueled new complaints from parents (in 2019, *The Handmaid's Tale* was on the American Library Association's Top 10 list of challenged books in the US), yet schools are resolute about teaching the novel and use it to discuss the dangers of censorship—in both Gilead and the real world.

Artistic freedom

In 2020, Margaret Atwood and other writers, journalists, and academics, signed an open letter to *Harper's Magazine* protesting about what they saw as cancel culture. It said: "As writers, we need a culture that leaves us room for experimentation, risk taking, and even making mistakes." While some see the exclusion of certain people from debate as the silencing of controversial opinions, others see it as the protection of marginalized groups from hate speech.

Offred, played by Elisabeth Moss, in the TV adaptation of *The Handmaid's Tale*

> 66 I made a rule for myself: I would not include anything that human beings had not already done in some other place or time, or for which the technology did not already exist. 99

Margaret Atwood, 2012

Beloved

---◊---

Toni Morrison
1987

Winner of the Pulitzer Prize in 1988, Toni Morrison's novel *Beloved* has long been celebrated for its visceral depiction of the brutality and trauma endured by enslaved people. But Morrison's graphic depiction of slavery has also made it one of the most challenged—and defended—books in US history.

Unflinching in its portrayal of America's history of slavery, *Beloved* contains vivid scenes of violence, bestiality, and murder. The story of a woman called Sethe, it switches between flashbacks of her pre-emancipation life on a plantation in Kentucky, and her post-emancipation life in Ohio, where she is haunted by one of her children, the "Beloved" of the title, whom she killed in order to save her from growing up in slavery.

A frequent complaint among parents is the "inappropriate sexual material" found in the novel—referring to multiple scenes of rape. However, most school boards rule that the novel's value in teaching students about slavery outweighs calls to remove the novel from classrooms. In 2006, a school district in Arlington Heights, Illinois, faced calls for a ban after a board member—who had not read the novel—cited a passage featuring acts of bestiality. Around 500 former and current students successfully protested the potential ban.

The novel's controversial sexual scenes came under scrutiny in 2016, when the state of Virginia introduced a bill—House Bill 516—requiring teachers to inform parents if school reading material contained explicit

Toni Morrison, 1982

sexual content. If parents were unhappy with their children reading the assigned text, alternatives had to be provided by the teacher. House Bill 516 soon came to be known as the "Beloved Bill," with Morrison's text frequently used as an example of a novel parents had the right to stop their children from reading. The bill was eventually vetoed because of its inflexibility and for encouraging school boards to read explicit scenes out of context.

> " Every dictator gets rid of the artist first ... They burn the books and execute the artist first ... Art might do something. It's dangerous. "

Toni Morrison

Spycatcher

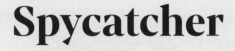

Peter Wright

1987

" These were genuine matters of public importance that the public should be allowed to know about. **"**

Donald Trelford, *The Observer*, 1988

Peter Wright (right) and his lawyer after winning the right to publish *Spycatcher* in Australia

In 1985, a former British intelligence officer, Peter Wright, was putting the final touches to a memoir called *Spycatcher*. There were rumors that it contained sensational details of assassination plots, an allegation that a high-ranking member of the British security services was a Soviet mole, and the revelation that 30 agents of the counterintelligence department of MI5 (Britain's Security Service) had been prepared to stage a coup to topple the 1974 Labour government.

The British government attempted to suppress publication. It tried unsuccessfully to take Wright to court in Australia, where he was then living, for violating the Official Secrets Act. In 1987, however, *Spycatcher* was published in the US and became a best seller around the globe—except in the UK, where the book and any excerpts were banned. In 1988, the British courts finally lifted the ban, on the grounds that publication abroad had rendered the injunction moot. The final blow for the British government came in 1991, when the European Court of Human Rights ruled that Britain had violated the Council of Europe's freedom of expression protocols by muzzling the press.

The Satanic Verses

Salman Rushdie

1988

At the end of the 1980s, *The Satanic Verses* by Mumbai-born British novelist Salman Rushdie ignited an epic battle between advocates of artistic freedom and Islam. The picaresque plot of the novel, which belongs to the genre of magical realism, centers on the adventures of two Indian men, Gibreel Farishta and Saladin Chamcha. On the way to London, their plane explodes in a terrorist attack but they miraculously survive, washing up on an English beach where Gibreel metamorphoses into an angel and Saladin a devil.

From this point on, a wild sequence of dreams and adventures unfolds—riffs on religious texts and the mythologies of European and Islamic cultures. Many Muslim people considered the novel blasphemous, perceiving a character named Mahound—a medieval variant of the name Muhammad—as a satirical portrait of the Prophet Muhammad. They were also offended by Rushdie's revival of a discredited tale from early Islamic history (allegedly recounted in lost Qur'anic verses, later dubbed "The Satanic Verses") in which Muhammad is tricked into accepting the divinity of three pagan goddesses (thus violating Islamic monotheism). The novel also features a dream sequence in which prostitutes take the names of Mahound's/Muhammad's wives.

66 If you start reading a book and you don't like it you always have the option of shutting it. At this point it loses its capacity to offend you. 99

Salman Rushdie, 2013

In February 1989, Iran's political and religious leader Ayatollah Khomeini issued a fatwa calling for Rushdie's assassination. A fatwa is a decree issued by a cleric with which observant Muslims must comply; it can only be repealed by the same cleric. As Khomeini died in June 1989, in theory the fatwa against Rushdie cannot be rescinded.

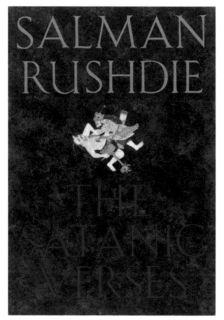

Cover of *The Satanic Verses*

> **❝ In this age we are asked to define ourselves by hate. ❞**
>
> **Salman Rushdie**, 2013

The novel was banned in India, Bangladesh, Sudan, South Africa, Sri Lanka, Kenya, Thailand, Tanzania, Indonesia, Singapore, and Venezuela. Rushdie went into hiding, was placed under armed police protection, and was forced to remain in hiding for at least a decade. Although Rushdie himself escaped physical harm, his Japanese translator was murdered, his Italian and Norwegian publishers were attacked, bookshops that stocked the novel were fire-bombed, and at least 59 people were killed around the world in protest riots. Devastated by the consequences of the fatwa, Rushdie, who was born a Muslim, issued a statement in December 1990, in which he affirmed "There is no God but Allah and Muhammad is his Prophet," the Muslim statement of faith. Unhappy about abandoning his free speech principles, Rushdie soon regretted making the statement.

The book and the violent aftermath of its publication became a proxy point of contention in the culture wars between Islam and the West, and also between Iran and Saudi Arabia, which were vying with each other for power within the Islamic world.

In 1998, the Iranian government amended the fatwa, stating that they would neither support nor hinder Rushdie's assassination. However, in 2012, 23 years after the original fatwa, Rushdie declined to attend an Indian literary festival due to police warnings of new, credible threats against him. *The Satanic Verses* is still unavailable in most of the countries that originally banned it, although South Africa lifted its ban on the novel in 2002.

Sued for libel

India's former Prime Minister Indira Gandhi appears as a character in Rushdie's 1981 novel *Midnight's Children*, a coming-of-age story set against the history of India's transition from British colonial rule to independence. Gandhi is portrayed as an evil widow who caused her husband's death. Deeply offended, Gandhi sued Rushdie for libel and won. In future editions, the character remained but the offending sentence was removed.

The Alchemist

Paulo Coelho

1988

A tale of spiritual discovery, *The Alchemist*, by Brazilian author Paulo Coelho, is about an Andalusian shepherd boy who travels through North Africa to Egypt in order to fulfill a prophetic dream. Translated into 83 languages, it became an international best seller, but it was the Farsi (Persian) translations that made global headlines.

In 2011, Coelho's Iranian publisher, Dr. Arash Hejazi, informed him that Iran's Ministry of Culture and Islamic Guidance had banned all of his books without explanation. In response, the pair published Coelho's works in Farsi online for free. At the same time, Coelho noted on his blog that his work had been available in Iran for 12 years, and that *The Alchemist* had sold some six million copies there.

Facing pressure from the Brazilian government and international media, the Iranian ambassador in Brazil claimed that the action had been taken against Hejazi's publishing house, Caravan Books, rather than Coelho. Two years previously, Hejazi had supported claims that government forces were responsible for the death of a female student during anti-government protests in Tehran. The ambassador claimed Hejazi, who had tried to save the woman's life, was a suspect in her death and accused him of manufacturing rumors of a ban on Coelho's work in order to discredit Iran's reputation. More than a decade later, it remains unclear whether Coelho's works are available in Iran.

Final Exit

◇

Derek Humphry
1991

Derek Humphry became an advocate for assisted dying during the terminal illness of his wife Jean, who had decided to end her life when her suffering became unbearable. Derek agreed to help her even though he risked arrest (ending one's own life is not a crime in the UK, where Derek and Jean were living, but helping someone else do so is). No one knew that Derek had helped his wife die until his book *Jean's Way*, an account of her illness and planned suicide, was published in 1978. The police decided not to prosecute as Humphry had been acting in accordance with Jean's wishes.

After his wife's death, Humphry moved to the US, where he set up the Hemlock Society (1980–2003) whose aim was to legalize assisted dying and help people with a terminal condition end their lives. To further the cause, he wrote *Final Exit*. Much of the book contains uncontroversial practical advice on planning for death by making a living will stipulating when life support should be withdrawn. However, it also contains explicit instructions for dying by suicide as painlessly as possible, including tables of drug dosages. Many people argued that the book was dangerous since it could be used by suicidal people who were not terminally ill.

The book was an instant success, reaching No.1 on *The New York Times* best seller list. Since many groups and individuals oppose euthanasia as a violation of the sanctity of life or see it as a potential infringement on disabled people's rights, the book was, and remains, controversial. It was impounded in Australia and temporarily banned in New Zealand until the Office of Indecent Publications could rule on its suitability. It is now available in both countries, but it is still banned in France. Humphry has responded by saying, "If people could get lawful euthanasia, my book would become unnecessary."

Wild Swans: Three Daughters of China

Jung Chang

1991

A sweeping and harrowing family history, *Wild Swans: Three Daughters of China* tells the true stories of three generations of women in 20th-century China. Yang Yu-fang (1909–1969), the writer's grandmother, became the concubine of a warlord general in the 1920s on the strength of her traditional "feminine virtues," such as her bound feet and zither-playing. Her daughter, Baoqing (born 1931), came of age during the Japanese occupation of China in World War II and the rise of communism. The author (born 1952), was a teenager at the start of Mao Zedong's Cultural Revolution (1966–1976), a brutal purge in which an estimated 2 million people were murdered or died of starvation. At the age of 14, Jung Chang briefly became a Red Guard, forced to go on violent house raids to root out class enemies.

The book ends with Jung Chang leaving China for Britain after Mao's death, which is where she wrote *Wild Swans*. The book, which contains damning indictments of Mao, fell victim to China's strict ban on biographies of political figures as soon as it was published and remains banned in mainland China, though it is available in Taiwan and Hong Kong. Other books by Jung Chang, including a biography of Mao (2005), are also banned, and to this day, the author is prohibited from entering China apart from two weeks each year to visit her aging mother. In Jung Chang's words, "History is the most dangerous subject in China."

" Once you ask questions, you immediately find that the propaganda and the myths don't add up. "

Jung Chang, 2019

American Psycho

Bret Easton Ellis
1991

In 1990, before *American Psycho* had even been published, author Bret Easton Ellis received death threats. Rumors concerning the book's graphic violence had begun to swirl in New York's literary circles and an article in *Time* magazine had made the controversy public knowledge.

Described as a black comedy, *American Psycho* follows Patrick Bateman, a Wall Street yuppie who is also a serial killer. Obsessed with his own image and success, Bateman, the first-person narrator, casually switches from talking about designer labels to describing in vivid detail the murders he commits, as well as acts of torture, mutilation, cannibalism, and necrophilia. Although women are his main targets, other murder victims include a colleague, a homeless man, and a child.

" Is evil something you are? Or is it something you do? "

Bret Easton Ellis, 1991

The original publishers, Simon & Schuster, canceled the book after many staff members and Ellis's usual cover artist flagged up the book's "disgusting" content. The company's CEO, Dick Snyder, said, "It went beyond the boundaries of acceptable taste."

When *American Psycho* was published by Vintage in 1991, the vitriol intensified. Believing the novel was "a how-to novel on the torture and dismemberment of women," the National Organization for Women called for boycotts of both Ellis's work and the publishing house. Readers also struggled to separate the protagonist from the author.

At the time of publication, only a few critics recognized the novel as a satire on capitalism and materialism in the US, as well as a subversion of the American Dream. Boosted by the film *American Psycho* (2000), the book became a cult novel and achieved recognition as a literary work. However, the explicit content remains problematic, and sales of *American Psycho* continue to be restricted around the world. In Australia and New Zealand, copies must be shrink-wrapped and can only be purchased by readers over the age of 18.

Shame

Taslima Nasrin

1993

Taslima Nasrin's novel *Shame* is about the aftermath of a real event—the destruction of the 470-year-old Babri Masjid mosque in the Indian city of Ayodhya by Hindu extremists on December 6, 1992. The mosque's demolition sparked violence between Muslims and Hindus in India, Pakistan, and Bangladesh.

Shame follows a Hindu family, the Duttas, living in Bangladesh, over a period of 13 days as they try to survive the terrifying wrath of Muslim rioters seeking vengeance for the mosque's destruction. It explores the different reactions of each member of the family, and condemns the Bangladeshi government's failure to protect the country's tiny Hindu minority.

Shame was published in Bengali in February 1993, and quickly sold around 60,000 copies. However, five months later, Bangladesh's government banned the novel for causing "misunderstandings among communities." An Islamic militant group also issued an unofficial fatwa against the author. Denouncing Nasrin for her "blasphemy and conspiracy against Islam," the group campaigned for her execution, burning effigies of her on the streets.

Taslima Nasrin, in France, where she was awarded the Simone de Beauvoir Prize, in 2008

Bangladesh's government failed to condemn the violence. Nasrin feared for her life but was unable to leave the country because her passport had been confiscated after she wrote newspaper articles condemning female oppression in the country.

Eventually Nasrin's passport was returned, and she escaped to Europe. She returned to Bangladesh a few months later, but her stay was short-lived. In June 1994, the government issued a warrant for her arrest after she criticized the Qur'an in an interview. Although the charges were eventually dropped, Nasrin was forced into exile again, first in Sweden and then in India.

> " My job is to write, which I will continue to do for as long as I live, even if I am not allowed to be read. "

Taslima Nasrin, 2012

The God of Small Things

Arundhati Roy

1997

When Arundhati Roy's debut novel *The God of Small Things* won the Man Booker Prize in 1997, the author became an international literary sensation. But some readers in her native Kerala, India, viewed the book as an attack on the state's government—the first democratically elected communist government in the world.

In a family saga that switches between the years 1969 and 1993, and contains elements of magic realism, Roy follows the fortunes of fraternal twins Rahel and Estha. It explores multiple themes, including Kerala's acceptance of the Hindu caste system while espousing an egalitarian ideology, and the legacy of imperialism. Roy claims that her inspiration was an image of an American car, a sky-blue Plymouth, stuck in a Marxist demonstration—a scene that crops up in chapter two.

Roy's detractors claimed one of the characters, Comrade Namboodiripad, the owner of a seedy hotel converted from his ancestral home, was a caricature of E. M. S. Namboodiripad, the father of communism in Kerala. Namboodiripad described the novel as pandering to anti-communist sentiments around the world.

The novel's sexual content also raised hackles. In 1997, a Kerala lawyer sued Roy for obscenity because of the sexually graphic description of the relationship between Amu, one of the main characters, and Velutha, who pays with his life for his transgression. *The God of Small Things* survived these attacks and was not censored in India. However, it was banned from a school in Gardendale, Alabama, in 2019, because of "inappropriate" sexual content.

" The Marxists worked from within the communal divides, never challenging them, never appearing not to. "

Arundhati Roy, 1997

His Dark Materials

Philip Pullman

1995–2000

British author Philip Pullman's Carnegie Prize–winning fantasy trilogy *His Dark Materials* tells the story of 13-year-old Lyra, a loyal and adventurous heroine. Lyra lives in Jordan College, Oxford, one of 23 scholastic sanctuaries of the Magisterium, the governing body of a supreme and evil church.

When Lyra's friend Roger goes missing, her quest to find him uncovers many secrets, from covert research into elemental particles called Dust to state-sanctioned kidnap to feed the Magisterium's experiments. In the course of her hunt, Lyra and a new friend called Will move between parallel universes, aided by an alethiometer (a truth-telling instrument that looks like a compass).

A host of fantastical beings and creatures populate the novels. Every person is accompanied by a "daemon"—a manifestation of their soul in animal form. The Authority—God—turns out to be an impossibly ancient and fragile fraud, and a motley cast of angels, scientists, polar bears, witches, and a former nun all work to either support or dismantle the Magisterium.

In addition to criticizing the way the Church seeks to control human destiny, the books call into question the gendering of sin. Mrs. Coulter, who kidnaps children for the Magisterium, is asked to capture and destroy her own daughter (revealed to be Lyra), whom the Magisterium believes will bring about a modern-day Fall from Eden. Instead of fulfilling the Magisterium's scheme, Mrs. Coulter saves her daughter, and Lyra saves Pullman's parallel universes with a life-affirming kiss shared with Will.

Philip Pullman has never made his antagonism toward the Church a secret. Most of his work focuses on a rewriting of Judeo-Christian origins and what he sees as the iniquitous nature of an all-powerful religion. Interviewed about *His Dark Materials* by *The Washington Post* in 2001, he said, "I'm trying to undermine the basis of Christian belief."

To begin with, religious objections to the themes of the novels were overshadowed by protests about the glorification of witchcraft in another young adult series of the late 1990s, J. K. Rowling's *Harry Potter* books (see pp. 164–165). Neither *Northern Lights* (1995), the first volume of Pullman's trilogy (published as *The Golden Compass* in the US) nor *The Subtle Knife* (1997), the second, appeared in the top 100 list of banned books in the 1990s. The first rumblings of disquiet began with the final and most controversial book, *The Amber Spyglass*, published in 2000. A British journalist labeled Pullman "the most dangerous author in Britain" in a 2002 article in the *Mail on Sunday*, and a writer in the *Catholic Herald* called the books "the stuff of nightmares" in 2003.

The furore truly began in 2007, when *His Dark Materials* made the Top 10 list of banned books published by the American Library Association (ALA). The trigger was the release of *The Golden Compass*, a film starring Nicole Kidman and Daniel Craig as

" Evil seeps out of the very things we are accustomed to find refuge in: parents, priests, and God himself. "

The Catholic Herald, 2003

" Everybody has the right to form their own opinion and read what they like and come to their own conclusion about it ... I trust the reader. "

Philip Pullman, 2007

Lyra's parents. Although many religious implications were removed from the film, which was heavily promoted to children, some school boards felt it could lead unwary parents to buy the trilogy for their children. Schools across Canada and the US pulled the books from their shelves, citing their anti-religious message.

By 2008, the entire trilogy ranked second on the ALA's list of banned books. One Canadian school retained the books, but added labels stating: "representations of the Church in this novel are purely fictional."

Christian groups were most disturbed by the fundamental questions raised by Pullman about the Fall (which is revealed as the defining moment of mankind, rather than the death of innocence) and the adult characters' ultimate declaration for atheism. The depiction of God as a frail being who dies in the final volume, as well as some of the dialogue—"Christian religion is ... a mistake" and "the truest proof of our love for God [is to] give him the gift of death"—were both cited as evidence of Pullman's true purpose: atheism for kids.

For many opponents of Pullman's work, the ban was considered a success; the other films in the trilogy were not made, and the books were controversial enough to take eighth place in the ALA's Top 100 list of banned books for the 2000s. However, with a critically acclaimed BBC adaptation of *His Dark Materials* covering the first and second volumes in 2019 and 2020, the battle may just be getting started.

Banned by the Church

In 1559, the Catholic Church published the *Index Librorum Prohibitorum* (*Prohibited Books*), a list of books banned on the grounds that they were scandalous or contained unorthodox ideas. The list was regularly updated from 1571, and by the 20th century contained some 5,000 titles. Some reversals did occur—all heliocentric works, for example, disappeared after 1758. In 1966, the Second Vatican Council, convened by Pope John XXIII to settle doctrinal issues, admitted it could not keep up with the flood of contemporary literature and ended publication of the list, making it morally but not spiritually binding.

The Harry Potter Series

J. K. Rowling

1997–2016

The fantastical world of wizards and witches in the *Harry Potter* series of books created by British author J. K. Rowling holds a special place in the hearts of millions of people. The story begins when Harry Potter, orphaned and miserable, is invited to attend Hogwarts, a school for witches and wizards. Here, Harry and his friends learn spells, make magic potions, play Quidditch—a competitive game on broomsticks—and gradually unravel the mystery of Harry's origins.

In addition to being translated into 60 languages, Rowling's seven-book series has spawned a beloved eight-movie franchise. Despite this success, the *Harry Potter* books have faced many challenges and bans—more than any other titles in the US between 2000 and 2005, according to the American Library Association. Most of these are instigated by conservative Christians opposed to witchcraft, which they claim promotes Satanism and the occult, as well as "anti-family themes." In 2019, the Reverend Dan Reehil of St. Edward Catholic School in Nashville, Tennessee, decried *Harry Potter* as "present[ing] magic as both good and evil, which is not true," claiming that he removed the books from the school's library after consulting with exorcists in the US and Rome. Elsewhere in the world, the books have been unsuccessfully challenged in Russia and banned in the UAE, again for their occult subject matter.

> " The curses and spells used in the books are actual curses and spells [which] risk conjuring evil spirits. "

Reverend Dan Reehil, St. Edward Catholic School, Nashville, 2019

The 21st Century

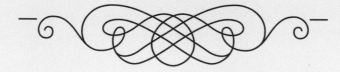

Persepolis

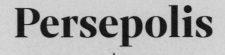

Marjane Satrapi

2000

" It's based on the story of my life, so it's not some stuff that is made up to make kids scared. These things exist in the world. "

Marjane Satrapi, 2013

Cover of the first edition of *Persepolis*, 2000

Marjane Satrapi's graphic novel *Persepolis*, first published in France in 2000–2003, paints a vivid picture of life in Iran between the start of the Islamic Revolution (1978) and the end of the Iran-Iraq war (1988). The memoir describes a turbulent period that Satrapi, the only child of Marxist parents and the great-granddaughter of one or Iran's last emperors, mines with great comic effect. The comedy is often very dark, and sometimes heartbreaking.

Persepolis was immediately banned in Iran. However, in 2013 Satrapi and the world were shocked to learn of an attempt to ban it in Chicago's public schools, especially as it was a text recommended by the National Council of Teachers of English. The ban led to campaigns on social media and protests outside high schools, including a "read-in" at one school. Under pressure, the Chicago Public Schools Association (CPS) backtracked, claiming that their intention had been to remove access to the book only by younger children. Despite the public outcry, *Persepolis* continues to be challenged by some American parents.

The Kite Runner

Khaled Hosseini

2003

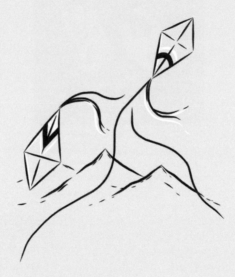

" There are things in the book that are of a serious nature, but I feel the kids have the intellectual capacity to deal with those things. "

Khaled Hosseini, 2013

When Khaled Hosseini's debut novel, *The Kite Runner*, was published in 2003 the Afghan-American author was praised for his compelling portrayal of Afghan history and culture. The novel became a commercial and critical success and joined other contemporary classics on US high school reading lists.

The story centers on two boys, Amir and Hassan, who are close friends, growing up in Kabul in the 1970s. Amir is the son of a wealthy and respected judge; Hassan the son of the man's servant, or so everyone is led to believe. The boys spend almost all their time together and love to fly kites. However, as they grow up their difference in status (Hassan belongs to the low-caste Hazara) begins to matter more, and Amir betrays Hassan.

The Kite Runner was banned in Afghanistan in 2008, after the film of the book came out in 2007, for "humiliating one of our ethnic groups." The movie also spawned parental objections to the book in US schools, mainly because of its sexual content, in particular a scene where Hassan is raped by a neighborhood bully. Although Hosseini is not graphic in his description, and the episode is a pivotal moment in the narrative, some parents and school boards think it is inappropriate for students. Other complaints concern the use of "profanities" in the novel and, for Muslims, the depiction of Islam as backward and cruel.

Most attempts to ban the book fail, but in 2017, the Higley Unified School District in Gilbert, Arizona, suddenly removed *The Kite Runner* from reading lists. Students were told that its suitability had not been properly assessed, but student journalists disproved this claim—noting that Hosseini's work had been assessed and approved when it was added to the curriculum five years previously. Subsequently, the school district accepted that it had not adhered to the official review process, but denied the book's removal had been an act of censorship.

A poster for the movie of *The Kite Runner*, released in 2007

The Bastard of Istanbul

Elif Shafak

2006

E lif Shafak's story of four generations of women living in Istanbul weaves together the past and present, Muslim Turks and Christian Armenians. Across a sprawling canvas that spans continents and generations, Shafak reunites a family shattered by history, and in so doing exposes its secrets and lies.

The book begins in Istanbul 20 years before the main action of the novel, when 19-year-old Zeliha Kazancı, a mini-skirted, high-heeled rebel in conservative Istanbul, is on her way to get an abortion. At the clinic, Zeliha undergoes a last-minute change of heart and decides to keep the child. The novel then fast-forwards to the present, when the child, Asya, is a young woman. She and

Zeliha, who has never revealed the identity of Asya's father, live with her grandmother, great-grandmother, and three eccentric aunts. The narrative then jumps to the story of another young woman, Armanoush, whose upbringing has been shared between her American mother, Rose, in Arizona, and her Armenian-American father in San Francisco. To spite her former husband and his family, Rose marries a Turkish man, Mustapha, who turns out to be the long-lost brother of the Kazancı family.

As she reaches adulthood, Armanoush's loyalties come to lie with her Armenian family. In an effort to come to terms with her past and to find out more about her Armenian grandmother's childhood in Istanbul, she decides to visit the city. Unbeknown to her parents, when she gets to Istanbul she stays with her step-father's Muslim family and gets to know Asya.

> " Our history, our stories lie here in the layers just beneath our feet. As a storyteller, it is my job to collect them. "

Elif Shafak, 2006

At the core of the novel is the Armenian genocide of 1915, in which a large percentage of Turkey's Armenian population—a Christian minority that had lived in the multiethnic Ottoman Empire for centuries—died. The novel reveals the brutality and horror of the genocide, which began with the rounding up and murder of Armenian intellectuals on April 24, 1915. The Ottoman government then forced the rest of the population to march south toward the Syrian desert under armed guard. Along the way, between 650,000 and one million people perished of exhaustion and starvation. The Turkish government grudgingly admits that some atrocities were committed but argues that it was a time of war and claims that few Armenians died during the march. The genocide was, however, well-documented and is a historical fact.

In Turkey, discussing the genocide is illegal under Article 301 of the Turkish Penal Code, which makes it a crime to "denigrate Turkishness," punishable by up to three years in prison. In Shafak's novel, Armanoush explicitly states her belief in the genocide when she says, "I am the grandchild of genocide survivors who lost all their relatives in the hands of Turkish butchers in 1915."

In 2006, a nationalist lawyer filed a complaint against Shafak for the words of her character. She joined 40 other writers he had attacked. After a 30-minute trial, Shafak was acquitted, but the furore drew angry attention from ultra-nationalists, who protested against the author in the streets, spitting on her picture. For 18 months, Shafak had to be protected by armed guards. Meanwhile, writers in Turkey are still at risk of prosecution under Article 301.

Shafak has also come under scrutiny for two other novels, *The Gaze* (2000) and *Three Daughters of Eve* (2016), which fell foul of a Turkish law against obscenity for their descriptions of child abuse and sexual harassment. At the time, Shafak noted: "Turkey has alarmingly high levels of sexual harassment, gender-based violence, and child brides. Instead of dealing with the problem, the authorities prosecute novelists." No charges were brought but Shafak, who now lives in London, fears harassment or worse if she visits Turkey. She has not been there for several years, even missing the funeral of the beloved grandmother who raised her while Shafak's mother completed her education.

No freedom for the press

Since a failed coup in 2016, press freedom in Turkey has been under sustained attack, with nearly 200 media outlets shut down. Turkey jails more journalists than any other country in the world, and the state has been implicated in the 2007 shooting and murder of Hrant Dink, a Turkish-Armenian publisher. Even the country's best-known novelist, Nobel Prize–winner Orhan Pamuk (left) has been sued for discussing the Armenian genocide.

> " In countries where there isn't freedom of speech, books matter. "

Elif Shafak, 2019

Cover of the first edition, 2006

Fun Home: A Family Tragicomic

Alison Bechdel

2006

Fun Home: A Family Tragicomic is a graphic novel and memoir by American cartoonist Alison Bechdel, famous for her *Dykes to Watch Out For* comic strip series. It chronicles Bechdel's life growing up in her family's funeral home business (or "fun home," as she and her siblings nicknamed it) in Pennsylvania. *Fun Home* explores her relationship with her emotionally distant and at times enraged father, who, she came to realize, was a closeted gay man. The impact of his death—which she concludes was a result of suicide—in her early adulthood, as well as her own emerging lesbian identity are two of the central themes in the book, a text that won multiple awards and was later adapted into a Tony Award–winning Broadway play.

As with many other famous LGBTQ+ books, *Fun Home* faced a homophobic backlash upon publication. In 2006, the year it was published, a woman in Marshall, Missouri, denounced the book as "pornography" and demanded that her local library remove it from their shelves, arguing that children would be attracted to its comic book format. The book was removed temporarily, but was eventually reinstated.

Fun Home also faced attempted bans at college level in Utah, South Carolina, and California. In South Carolina, the state legislature reacted to its inclusion on a summer reading list for incoming students at the College of Charleston by attempting to cut funding to the following year's reading program. This failed, but the legislature succeeded in redirecting the funding to support books about the US Constitution.

> " Sexual shame is in itself a kind of death. "

Alison Bechdel, 2006

Alison Bechdel being photographed for *Out* magazine in 2012

The Absolutely True Diary of a Part-Time Indian

Sherman Alexie

2007

Aimed at young adults, Indigenous American Sherman Alexie's *The Absolutely True Diary of a Part-Time Indian* is a humorous, and unsparing, memoir about growing up on the Spokane Indian Reservation in Washington state.

The book was one of the most challenged works in the US for nearly a decade. Some people argued that it was unsuitable for young readers because it included bullying, masturbation, and violence. Others felt that topics such as alcoholism and poverty depicted Indigenous American communities in a negative light, or they found it racist or culturally insensitive. New objections to the work were raised in 2018, when Alexie was accused of using his status as one of the best-known Indigenous authors to sexually harass women.

Other Indigenous authors in the US have also been criticized for their realistic depictions of Indigenous lives, while *Rethinking Columbus: The Next 500 Years* (1998), an anthology of work that reevaluates the impact of Christopher Columbus, has been challenged for its criticism of Europeans who committed genocide against Indigenous people and forced those remaining on to reservations. Many Indigenous authors are faced with a predicament: if they write accurately about their history and their lives, some non-Indigenous readers will challenge such depictions and attempt to ban their work.

" Book banners want to control debate and limit the imagination. I encourage debate and celebrate imagination. "

Sherman Alexie

The Cartoons that Shook the World

Jytte Klausen

2009

Danish-born Jytte Klausen's *The Cartoons that Shook the World* examines the international furore that erupted in 2005 when the Danish newspaper *Jyllands-Posten* published 12 caricatures of the Prophet Muhammad. Islam considers physical representations of the Prophet blasphemous, and the cartoons' publication had led to violent riots and more than 250 deaths worldwide.

Klausen's primary purpose was not to rake over arguments concerning freedom of expression and the right to offend, but to examine the real motives of those who stoked the conflict. She argues that politicians on both sides of the fight sought to whip up emotions in order to inflame preexisting conflicts. Their aims were to gain support in upcoming elections in Denmark and Egypt, and later to destabilize governments in countries such as Pakistan, Libya, and Nigeria.

Klausen planned to include in her book an image of the newspaper page featuring the 12 cartoons. However, after asking "expert advice," her publisher, Yale University Press, decided that this could instigate violence, damage US foreign policy, and threaten the safety of the author. Klausen agreed to the removal of the cartoons on the condition that a note saying they had been censored was included in the book. When Yale tried to bargain with Klausen, offering to show her the dossier of expert advice if she accepted the censorship without comment, she refused. The book was published without the cartoons but with a note acknowledging that censorship had taken place, causing an outcry among many fellow authors and academics.

Melissa
(formerly George)

Alex Gino

2015

This children's novel tells the story of a young transgender American girl, Melissa, who is in the fourth grade and has not yet told anyone she is a girl. The rest of her school views her as a boy named George, which complicates her life even more when she wants to audition for the role of Charlotte, the wise spider who saves her friend Wilbur the pig, in her school's production of *Charlotte's Web*. Melissa steps into her truest self, not just to be in the play, but to be seen and respected for who she really is.

The book has made the American Library Association's Top 10 Most Challenged Books list every year since its publication, reaching the No. 1 spot in 2018, 2019, and 2020, mainly coming under attack from anti-trans campaigners for its depiction of a transgender child. In addition to these challenges, trans activists took issue with the original title of the book, *George*, because it deadnamed the main character— used her birth name (George) rather than the one she chose (Melissa). In November 2021, the author, themselves genderqueer, announced that the book would be reissued under the title *Melissa* from April 2022.

The Hate U Give

Angie Thomas

2017

Acoming-of-age novel that tackles teenage angst and police brutality in modern-day America, *The Hate U Give* was inspired by the tragic shooting of Oscar Grant, an unarmed Black man, and the Black Lives Matter movement. Its author, Mississippi native and former rapper Angie Thomas, wanted to write a story that showcased the hardships of Black American lives.

The novel follows Starr, a 16-year-old Black girl, who attends an all-white private school. She becomes a mouthpiece for racial inequality in her home community after witnessing the shooting of her friend Khalil by a police officer when the pair are pulled over while driving home from a party. The story touches on themes such as "code switching" (when a person of color switches their language and behavior to assimilate in white spaces), racial tensions, and inequitable justice.

In 2018, *The Hate U Give* caught the attention of Katy Independent School District in Texas. Parents complained about the use of explicit language in the book, and it was subsequently banned from schools in the state. However, the ban was widely criticized by the

> ❝ And at the end of the day, you don't kill someone for opening a car door. If you do, you shouldn't be a cop. ❞

The Hate U Give, 2017

Angie Thomas, 2017

public and the book was eventually reinstated, though students could only borrow it with parental permission. In 2018, a police advocacy group in Mount Pleasant, South Carolina, also tried to ban the book in high schools, as they believed it promoted an anti-police message. However, all attempts to censor the book were eventually overturned. The book became a huge success, and a film adaptation of the novel, released in 2018, also received widespread popular and critical acclaim.

Killing Commendatore

Haruki Murakami

2018

Best-selling Japanese author Haruki Murakami's 14th novel *Killing Commendatore* is quirky and fantastical, and has explicit sex scenes, much like his other internationally popular novels. In 2018, however, it was singled out by Hong Kong's Obscene Articles Tribunal on charges of "indecency"—defined by the tribunal as including "violence, depravity, and repulsiveness." Though not as serious as "obscene," which results in an immediate ban, this meant

" You have to go through the darkness before you get to the light. "

Haruki Murakami

that the book could only be sold to people aged 18 or over and every copy had to be sealed in cellophane, with a warning that it contained material that "could offend." Chinese translations of the novel immediately disappeared from the Hong Kong Book Fair, which was in progress at the time.

Why the Hong Kong tribunal picked on this particular novel by Murakami is unclear. One explanation is that in 2014 the author sent a message of support to activists protesting against what they saw as an undemocratic election reform plan drafted for Hong Kong by Beijing. This was Murakami's first novel since that event.

I Hate Men

Pauline Harmange
2020

Threats to ban a book often have the opposite effect—they boost sales. This is what happened when French writer Pauline Harmange's treatise on "misandry," *I Hate Men*, originally published as a 96-page essay by micropublisher Monstrograph, attracted the attention of Ralph Zurmély, an adviser to the French gender equality ministry. According to the ministry, Zurmély had read only the title and publisher's description, but he threatened legal action against Monstrograph if it continued to publish the essay. He asserted that incitement to hatred on the basis of sex was a criminal offense.

In *I Hate Men*, Harmange argues that hating men is an understandable and moral conclusion based on women's collective experiences of men's violence. She points out that men are responsible for the vast majority of sexual violence and domestic assaults, and argues that when women are not trying to appease and reassure men, they are free to pursue more joyful pursuits. Asked about her book in a 2021 interview, she said, "Misandry is not a tool for feminism; it's just a reaction for what we are suffering every day."

Zurmély's reaction to *I Hate Men* ensured that it reached more eyes and ears. A major publisher, Éditions du Seuil, agreed to publish it when Monstrograph, which was run by volunteers, became overwhelmed by demand. The work went on to attract international interest and sales.

Cover of the French edition

moi
les hommes,
je les déteste

pauline
harmange

Stamped: Racism, Antiracism, and You

Ibram X. Kendi and Jason Reynolds

2020

Historian Ibram X. Kendi's 2016 book *Stamped from the Beginning, The Definitive History of Racist Ideas in America* is a call for Americans to examine and then unlearn the racism present since the earliest years of their nation. To reach a younger audience, Kendi persuaded author Jason Reynolds to rewrite his book for teens and pre-teens. The resulting remix has been No. 2 on the American Library Association's list of banned and challenged books in both 2020 and 2021. Some parents in Maryland, New Jersey, and Texas have called for it to be removed from schools because they say it contains "selective storytelling incidents" and does not deal with racism against all people.

As in Kendi's original work, the book profiles five American thinkers (Puritan preacher Cotton Mather, founding father Thomas Jefferson, abolitionist William Lloyd Garrison, scholar W. E. B. Dubois, and Black activist Angela Davis) who have shaped the debate between racists and anti-racists, assimilationists and segregationists, explaining these terms in an engaging way that kids can understand. Reynolds has said that some parents object to the book because they do not want to have complicated conversations with their children. Yet, these are the conversations that kids are often most interested in having.

***Stamped* authors** Ibram X. Kendi (left) and Jason Reynolds

" The heartbeat of racism is denial, and the history in *Stamped* will not be denied, nor will young people's access to this book be canceled. "

Ibram X. Kendi, 2020

This Is a Swedish Tiger

Aron Flam

2020

In 2020, the Swedish-Jewish comedian Aron Flam published a controversial book called *Det är en svensk tiger* (*This Is a Swedish Tiger*), a satirical reference to the country's World War II slogan "*en svensk tiger*." Meaning both "a Swedish tiger" and "a Swede stays quiet," the slogan and its accompanying blue-and-yellow stylized tiger had reminded Swedes not only to be strong like a tiger, but to keep secrets and stay out of a war that was thought to have nothing to do with Sweden. After the war, however, it became clear that the Swedish government had been far from neutral.

Flam's book reveals the extent of Sweden's collaboration with the Nazis. For the cover, he chose a similar-looking tiger giving a Nazi salute and wearing a swastika armband. After becoming aware of the book, the Swedish government stopped a second print run and took legal action against Flam, on the spurious grounds that the image was protected by copyright. The defense lawyers argued that the image was satirical and Flam was found not guilty. Not only did the trial publicize Flam's book, but it also drew attention to Sweden's role in World War II.

1000 Years of Joys and Sorrows

Ai Weiwei

2021

U pon its publication in November 2021, international artist Ai Weiwei's long-anticipated memoir *1000 Years of Joys and Sorrows* faced an immediate ban in his native China. It was fully expected. Ai Weiwei's blog had been shut down in 2009, and in 2011, the artist had been detained in a secret location for 81 days.

After three decades of using innovative art in multiple forms to raise awareness of injustice all over the world, Ai Weiwei has become one of the most influential Chinese artists of his time. His targets are broad, as in *Perspective on Tiananmen Square* (1995), in which he derides worldwide symbols of state power, and specific, as in *Straight* (2008–2012), which incorporates steel rods recovered from a school that collapsed during the 2008 Sichuan earthquake, killing more than 5,000 children, a tragedy Ai Weiwei attributes to corrupt building inspectors.

Ai Weiwei once wrote, "I wouldn't say I've become more radical: I was born radical." Crown, his US publisher, acknowledged this by publishing a volume of selected poems by his father, Ai Qing (1910–1996) at the same time as *1000 Years of Joys and Sorrow*. Ai Qing's work gave the faceless masses in Mao's China a voice. His most famous poem, "Da Yan He" (1933), is a mournful paean to a wet nurse who drowned her infant daughter in order to raise another family's son.

Ai Qing's political views and activism led to the family being exiled to a hard-labor camp in Xinjiang for "mental correction for wrong thought." The pairing of Ai Weiwei's and Ai Qing's work shows how the son is carrying on his father's legacy of art as moral action.

Index

Acknowledgments

Toucan Books

Editorial Director Ellen Dupont; **Editor** Dorothy Stannard; **Designer** Dave Jones; **Consultants** B. J. Epstein, Robert Patterson; **Picture Researcher** Sharon Southren; **Researcher** Benjamin Hartnell-Booth; **Authenticity Readers** Stephanie Cohen, Kit Heyam, Philippa Willitts; **Proofreader** Julie Brooke; **Indexer** Marie Lorimer

Authors

Elizabeth Blakemore, Mary Frances Budzik, Aparna Dharwadker, B. J. Epstein, Autumn Green, Mark Collins Jenkins, Tim Harris, Tianyun Hua, Andrew Kerr-Jarrett, Janaka Lewis, Pas Pascali, Ana Cristina Peralta, Brian Robinson, Rick Smith, Betty Sun, Shannon Webber

Picture Credits

10 Getty Images: Christophel Fine Art / Contributor / Universal Images Group. **15 Alamy Stock Photo:** North Wind Picture Archives. **17 Getty Images:** The Print Collector / Contributor / Hulton Archives. **27 Getty Images:** Heritage Images / Contributor / Hulton Archives. **31 Alamy Stock Photo:** Pictorial Press Ltd. **33 Library of Congress, Washington, D.C.:** LC-DIG-ppmsca-07143. **35 Alamy Stock Photo:** Photo 12. **38 Library of Congress, Washington, D.C.:** LC-USZ62-88790. **40 Alamy Stock Photo:** North Wind Picture Archives. **43 Alamy Stock Photo:** Alpha Stock. **49 Alamy Stock Photo:** Lebrecht Music & Arts. **55 Retro AdArchives/ Penguin Random House. 59 Alamy Stock Photo:** INTERFOTO. **62 Alamy Stock Photo:** Retro AdArchives. **65 Courtesy of Between the Covers Rare Books, New Jersey. 66 Getty Images:** Anthony Barboza / Contributor / Archive Photos. **67 Alamy Stock Photo:** Granger Historical Picture Archive. **71 Alamy Stock Photo:** INTERFOTO. **79 Getty Images:** ullstein bild Dtl. / Contributor. **81 SuperStock:** Album / Oronoz. **83 Getty Images:** Bettmann / Contributor. **85 Alamy Stock Photo:** The Protected Art Archive/Penguin Random House LLC. **89 Shutterstock.com:** Carl Mydans / The LIFE Picture Collection. **93 Getty Images:** Schewe / ullstein bild / Contributor. **95 TopFoto. 97 Getty Images:** Archive Photos / Stringer. **101 Getty Images:** David Attie / Contributor / Michael Ochs Archives. **103 Alamy Stock Photo:** Granger Historical Picture Archive. **107 Getty Images:** LMPC / Contributor. **109 Getty Images:** LMPC / Contributor. **113 Library of Congress, Washington, D.C.:** LOC-LC-USZ62-119478. **115 Getty Images:** Carl T. Gossett, Jr. / New York Times Co. / Contributor. **119 Alamy Stock Photo:** Stephen Parker. **125 Bridgeman Images:** © Museum of Fine Arts, Houston / The Target Collection of American Photography, museum purchase funded by Target Stores. **129 Alamy Stock Photo:** ZUMA Press, Inc. **133 Alamy Stock Photo:** INTERFOTO. **137 Penguin Random House LLC. 138 Getty Images:** Tolga Akmen / Contributor / AFP. **139 Shutterstock.com:** George Kraychyk / MGM / Hulu / Kobal. **141 Getty Images:** Reg Innell / Contributor / Toronto Star. **143 Getty Images:** John Nobley / Fairfax Media Archives / Contributor. **146 Getty Images:** Culture Club / Contributor / Hulton Archive / Penguin Random House LLC. **147 Getty Images:** STF / Staff / AFP. **152 American Psycho by Bret Easton Ellis. Pan Macmillan/ Reproduced with permission of the Licensor through PLSclear. 155 Getty Images:** Raphael GAILLARDE / Contributor / Gamma Rapho. **167 © Marjane Satrapi & L'Association, 2000. 169 Alamy Stock Photo:** AA Film Archive. **172 Alamy Stock Photo:** ITAR-TASS News Agency. **173 Penguin Random House. 175 Getty Images:** M. Sharkey / Contributor / Contour RA. **181 Shutterstock.com:** Rogelio V Solis / AP. **183 Coline Pierré & Martin Page. 185 Getty Images:** Michael Loccisano / Staff.

All other images © Dorling Kindersley
For further information see: www.dkimages.com